PROFESSIONALS AND THE NEW MANAGERIALISM IN THE PUBLIC SECTOR

PROFESSIONALS AND THE NEW MANAGERIALISM IN THE PUBLIC SECTOR

Edited by
Mark Exworthy and Susan Halford

OPEN UNIVERSITY PRESS
Buckingham · Philadelphia

Open University Press
Celtic Court
22 Ballmoor
Buckingham
MK18 1XW

email: enquiries@openup.co.uk
world wide web: http://www.openup.co.uk

and
325 Chestnut Street
Philadelphia, PA 19106, USA

First Published 1999

A catalogue record of this book is available from the British Library

ISBN   0 335 19819 8 (pb)   0 335 19820 1 (hb)

Library of Congress Cataloging-in-Publication Data
Professionals and the new managerialism in the public sector / edited by Mark
    Exworthy and Susan Halford.
        p.   cm.
    "The idea for this book originated from a seminar series funded by the Faculty
of Social Sciences at the University of Southampton . . . this support . . . enabled
the contributors to present earlier versions of their papers at a one day
conference"—Acknowl.
    Includes bibliographical references and index.
    ISBN   0-335-19820-1   (hardcover). – ISBN   0-335-19819-8   (pbk.)
    1. Organizational change–Great Britain.   2. Government productivity–Great
Britain.   3.   Administrative agencies–Great Britain–Management.   4.
Professional employees in government–Great Britain.   I. Exworthy, Mark,
1966–   II. Halford, Susan.
JN329.073P76   1998
352.3'0941–dc21   98-13170
                                                                                    CIP

Copy-edited and typeset by The Running Head Limited, London and Cambridge
Printed in Great Britain by Biddles Ltd, Guildford and King's Lynn

Contents

Notes on contributors

Mark Exworthy is a Research Fellow at the Institute for Health Policy Studies at the University of Southampton. His principal research interests relate to the spatial impact of health policies, quasi-markets in health care and managerial roles in clinical effectiveness policies.

Susan Halford is a Lecturer in Sociology at the University of Southampton. Her recent research has involved in-depth investigations of the relationships between gender, organization and identity. She is co-author (with Mike Savage and Anne Witz) of *Gender, Careers and Organisations* (Macmillan, 1997), as well as of a number of other papers on this subject.

Gordon Causer is a Lecturer in Sociology at the University of Southampton. His main research interests lie in the field of work, employment and social inequality. His recent publications include 'Management and the control of technical labour' in *Work, Employment and Society* (1996), with Carol Jones.

Rob Flynn is a Reader in Sociology at the University of Salford. His research has been in the fields of urban sociology, social policy, health policy and management. His publications include *Structures of Control in Health Management* (Routledge, 1992), and he is joint author of *Markets and Networks: Contracting in Community Health Services* (Open University Press, 1996) and co-editor of *Contracting for Health* (Oxford University Press, 1997).

Stephen Harrison is a Reader in Health Policy and Politics at the Nuffield Institute for Health, University of Leeds. His interests include the micro- and macro-politics of health care. He has published on NHS personnel, management and policy. He is joint author of *Controlling Health Professionals* (Open University Press, 1994) and *Just Managing: Power and Culture in the NHS* (Macmillan, 1992).

Chris Jones is Professor of Social Policy and Social Work in the Department of Sociology, Social Policy and Social Work at the University of Liverpool. Since 1979 he has been particularly interested in exploring and writing about the impact of 'new right' social policy and ideology on British social work education. Recent publications include 'British social work and the classless society: the failure of a profession' in *Towards a Classless Society?*, edited by Helen Jones (Routledge, 1997) and 'The case against CCETSW' in *Issues in Social Work Education* (1997).

Pauline Leonard is a Research Fellow in the Department of Sociology and Social Policy at the University of Southampton. Her research interests are in the field of gender, identity and organization. She is currently conducting research in the National Health Service.

Ian Menter is Head of the School of Education at the University of North London. Previously he was Head of Research and Staff Development in the Faculty of Education at the University of the West of England. In the 1970s and 1980s he taught in primary schools in Bristol.

Yolande Muschamp is a Lecturer in Education in the Department of Education at the University of Bath. Her recent research includes the work of teachers, the management of primary schools in relation to marketization and a national assessment of Key Stage 2 testing for 11-year-olds. She is a joint author of *Work and Identity in the Primary School* (Open University Press, 1997).

Acknowledgements

The idea for this book originated from a seminar series funded by the Faculty of Social Sciences at the University of Southampton. We are grateful for this support as it enabled the contributors to present earlier versions of their papers at a one-day conference. In turn, we appreciate the effort made by the contributors to the conference and to the chapters in this book.

1 | Professionals and managers in a changing public sector: conflict, compromise and collaboration?

Mark Exworthy and Susan Halford

Introduction

Popular and academic discourse often take for granted the notion that managers and professionals are different. It is commonly assumed that the work managers do is quite distinct from that of professionals. This notion supposes that managers are committed to running bureaucracies, to establishing and applying rules. In this scenario, managers depend for their power and authority on their position in the bureaucratic hierarchy and on their knowledge of organizational politics and practice, acquired through experience in a particular organization. By contrast, professionals are thought to be committed to the provision of expert services and advice, and to depend for their power and authority on specialist knowledge which supersedes the confines of any single organization. Moreover, from the differences in occupational tasks, a range of differences in personal attributes and dispositions is assumed to follow. Traditionally, managers have been seen as conformist, self-interested and career motivated; whereas professionals have often been seen as more creative, altruistic and driven by ethical commitment to their expertise, or at least, by commitment to their profession as a way of securing status and privilege. An obvious conclusion from this stylized picture is that *relations between* managers and professionals will be marked by antipathy or even outright conflict.

Of course, this is a pastiche of both popular and academic images. Critical theoretical debates have long considered the complexities involved in distinguishing managerial work from professional work (see for example Larson 1977; Goldthorpe 1982; Savage *et al.* 1992). Empirical evidence has also suggested that the roles are rather more blurred than the stereotypes suggest. For instance, professionals working in the public sector have commonly built careers in single organizations and moved into managerial roles as they climb the ladder. In some cases, for example in local government, the managerial cadre has been composed almost entirely of professionals, sometimes known as 'bureau-professionals' (Newman and Clarke 1994) or 'managerial-professionals' (Laffin and Young 1990; also Causer and Exworthy in this volume).

Notwithstanding these complexities, a distinction between managers and professionals remains a persistent theme within popular and academic debate (for example Crompton 1990; Savage *et al.* 1992). Indeed, it is a theme which has acquired particular prominence in contemporary analyses of the public sector, where there has been a widespread and forceful emergence of new forms of managerialism over the past decade (see p. 6 below for further details). The new managerialism has far-reaching implications for the organization of professional work in the public sector. It has been interpreted by some as a strategic weapon with which to curb the powers of overly independent professionals and to challenge the monopoly of the bureau-professionals (for example see Stewart and Stoker 1989; Clarke *et al.* 1994; Leach *et al.* 1994; Farnham and Horton 1996). New forms of managerialism are represented (for example by Osbourne and Gaebler 1994) as an opportunity to take over from old-fashioned, bureaucratic managers unable to deal with despotic professionals and to inject the entrepreneurial vigour required to meet the needs of the public sector in the 1990s and beyond. Even in less conspiratorial accounts the new managerialism is seen to mark a critical juncture in relations between professional and managerial staff. For example, Newman and Clarke argue that '[m]anagement . . . was the agency which inherited the task of dismantling the old regimes and providing a new regime . . . around which organizations could be structured' (1994: 23), while Clarke *et al.* suggest that 'managerialization constitutes the means through which the structure and culture of public services is being re-cast' (1994: 4).

In times of such change, taken-for-granted practices and privileges of both management and professions may become more obvious as previously accepted arrangements are contested, defended or reworked (Reed 1989; Evetts 1992). In the process, new arrangements or accommodations may be wrought. Hence recent changes in the public sector offer an ideal opportunity to investigate the nature of 'professionalism' and 'managerialism' and the nature of the relations between professionals and managers. In particular, the aim of the collection of chapters in this book is to investigate the impact of new managerialist discourses, policy interventions and changing everyday practice on professionals and professionalism in the public sector. We have two major objectives. First, to explore the interactions which are taking place between *different* groups of professionals and managers in the public sector today. Rather than assuming a universal antagonism, we begin with the premise that relations between professionals and managers are constituted unevenly between and within different organizations. Thus, as well as conflict between professionals and managers in today's 'managerializing' public sector, which might most obviously be expected, this book actively seeks to establish whether there is also compromise and collaboration. Our second major objective is to consider the theoretical implications of these changing professional/managerial dynamics in the public sector. Although we begin with a specific empirical focus (changes in the public sector), important theoretical questions about the nature and future of professions and professionals emerge within the context of new managerialist developments in the public sector.

In the remainder of this chapter we offer a broad-brush overview of those recent changes in the public sector which we consider most significant for this analysis. We also briefly examine various explanations for these changes, making links between specific explanations and changing professional/managerial dynamics. Although some of these points will be elaborated in subsequent chapters, this initial overview frees our contributors from repeating the general contextual framework in each chapter, enabling them to develop their in-depth analyses of managers and professionals in particular parts of the public sector. Finally in this chapter we outline in detail the empirical and theoretical concerns which have led us to bring this collection together and which the authors endeavour to address.

A changing public sector

The history of the public sector is one of constant change. Major structural changes are regularly introduced in individual sub-sectors[1] with impacts upon statutory responsibilities and funding arrangements. Incremental changes are also frequently initiated at sub-sectoral and organizational levels. However, even in this general context, the 1980s and 1990s have marked a period of dramatic transformation right across the public sector, with fundamental implications for the structures, cultures and practices of its constituent sub-sectors and individual organizations. Particularly significant changes have included the imposition of new arrangements for financial accountability and the measurement of 'effectiveness'; the 'marketization' of structural arrangements between those who provide welfare services and those who pay for them; the 'marketization' of relations *within* service organizations; and attempts to change established relations between service providers and consumers. Each has potentially major implications for the constitution of 'managerialism' and 'professionalism' in the public sector, and for relations between public sector managers and professionals.

A central theme underpinning much recent change has concerned financial accountability and effectiveness. Beginning with Thatcherism, new understandings were promulgated by central government regarding the principles and practices of financial management in the public sector. Informed by monetarist theories, a reduction in public expenditure was touted as the principal objective of public sector restructuring in the 1980s. In fact, the apocalyptic budget cuts prophesied have failed to materialize (Clarke *et al.* 1994) and real expenditure on public services actually rose in the period from 1979 to 1992 (Farnham and Horton 1996). Despite this, concerns with financial accountability and effectiveness have had a dramatic impact on the vocabulary and indeed the underlying principles of public sector organization. The clearest example of this has been the 'marketization' of public services. Of course, public services have always operated within global budgets which have necessitated decisions about resource allocations, but recent changes involve a commitment to costing and pricing public services' activities in far greater detail than ever before (Miller 1992). In turn, this has enabled the introduction of cost-led competition within the public sector. Early examples of this affected ancillary services such as catering, cleaning and laundry services in local government and the NHS. Where previously these services were performed by staff employed *directly* by local authorities or health authorities (Painter 1991; Goodwin and Pinch 1995), the imposition of compulsory competitive tendering (CCT) opened them up to bids from any provider in the public or private sector. The presumption was that 'in-house' provision was inefficient because it did not have to be competitive. CCT established the principle that the public sector should not necessarily be the sole provider of services although it would, for the most part, continue to fund them and regulate the (quasi-) markets in which they operated (Le Grand and Bartlett 1993). This laid the foundations for subsequent policies.

Perhaps the most ambitious extension of this logic has been the so-called 'purchaser–provider split' in the NHS. Prior to 1991, health authorities were responsible for allocating resources to local services and also for managing those services. However, it was alleged that '[c]onflating the purchaser and provider functions in a single organization . . . [resulted in] a potential conflict of interest between the preferences of providers on the one hand and those of users on the other' (Hunter 1994: 6); so in 1991 the two functions were split. Health authorities became responsible for determining the needs of the local population and contracting with (public or private sector) providers to meet those needs. Service providers (hospitals and community health units) became responsible for managing the provision of services. Purchasers were not required to only contract with the most local provider. Indeed, the intention was that multiple providers would compete for contracts, encouraging more cost-effective and efficient services. Patients were also given a higher profile by these reforms. Notionally, 'money would follow patients' as they exercised their choice between providers of a given service. Like other reforms across the public sector, this involved a redefinition of the role of consumers vis-à-vis public services. Both central government and service users have often criticized public services as unresponsive, inflexible and run principally for the benefit of those who work for them (Farnham and

Horton 1996). This criticism has been levelled not only at managers but at professionals too, whose claim always to know what was best for users (who should be deferential to those professionals) has been increasingly disputed (Farnham and Horton 1996). The redefinition of users into 'customers' promised to enhance their status, offer greater choice and ensure responsiveness to individual needs.

Despite the Labour government's commitment to abolish the marketization 'flagship' (the internal market within the NHS), market principles continue to be extended in various ways across the public sector. For example, professional functions (such as legal and financial services) in local authorities have recently been subjected to CCT although the process relating to clinical services in the NHS has thus far been limited (Appleby 1995). Inside public sector organizations, financial decentralization has established 'customer–provider' relations between departments. Here, discrete functions (for example computer services and administrative support) command financial transactions between decentralized units. Thus the internal spaces of public sector organizations are constituted as 'accountable spaces' and placed in marketized relations with one another. Miller (1992) suggests that the creation of these *accountable* spaces facilitates the establishment of more *manageable* spaces. The development of cost-centres allows abstract spaces inside organizations to become 'calculable' and therefore comparable: 'calculative technologies make it possible to render visible [the] activities of individuals, to calculate the extent to which they depart from norm of performance and to accumulate such calculations in computers and files and to compare them' (p. 68). This makes possible the extension of managerial techniques and managerial controls over professionals, among others.

Entrepreneurial considerations have also been increasingly prioritized *within* the newly created and quasi-autonomous cost-centres and business units, as staff took on newly devolved responsibilities and, more pervasively still, adopted newly valued entrepreneurial attitudes and behaviours (du Gay 1996a). Such entrepreneurialism has also become a necessary part of public sector organizations' relations with the outside world, as competition for customers and income necessitates new public relations and marketing strategies (Flynn *et al.* 1997).

Thinking specifically about professionalism and managerialism, and relations between managers and professionals, two broad themes emerge from consideration of this recent public sector restructuring. First, there has clearly been a widespread shift in the *legitimacy* of management in the public sector. Calls for the introduction of general (i.e. non-professional) management can be traced back as far as the 1920s in some parts of the public sector (see Laffin and Young 1996 on local government), but in the past these have been effectively stalled by continued arguments in favour of professional control and autonomy. However, from the early 1980s onwards, it had become clear that calls for managerialization in the public sector were more widespread and forceful than ever before, and posed such a fundamental challenge to established practice that the professional paradigm might really be threatened this time (Day and Klein 1983; Leach *et al.* 1994). One factor which made this challenge more significant than previous occasions was the *variety of agencies* endorsing managerialization.

Central, of course, was the election of successive Conservative governments committed to bringing a 'wayward' public sector under 'proper' control, and vesting powers in managers who would 'do the right thing' (Newman and Clarke 1994; see also Jones in this volume). However, endorsement has also come from elements within service agencies themselves, where a new emphasis on the need for modern corporate management has been commonly expressed. Some individual professionals and managers were enthused and empowered by such possibilities (Hoggett 1991; Lowndes and Stoker 1992). Popular discourse has also endorsed the need for strong management in the public sector. Think, for example, of popular management guru John Harvey Jones's television programmes about NHS hospital management in Bradford, or consider the widespread resonance of Griffiths' remark that 'if Florence Nightingale were alive today she would be wandering the hospital corridors trying to find out who was in charge (Department of Health 1983: 22).

Coupled with marketization, this new emphasis on managerialism seems to place public sector managers in a position of unparalleled power and authority. It was not only that problems with existing arrangements had been identified, or simply that new structures or cadres of personnel were introduced which would supposedly rectify these supposed deficiencies. More than this, central government and sections of public sector agencies invested faith in *managers*, and in the language, techniques and values of *managerialism*, as the only way actually to deliver change.

The second key point is equally significant, and acts to qualify the first. The *version* of 'managerialism' being endorsed was quite distinct from previously established forms of management. Traditionally, the public sector has been characterized by Taylorist management, described as bureaucratic, inflexible, conformist and principally concerned with control and cost cutting (Pollitt 1993; Walby and Greenwell 1994). By contrast, the *new* managerialism emphasized innovation, creativity and empowerment. The new managers are policy 'entrepreneurs', highly motivated, resourceful, and able to shift the frame of reference beyond established norms and procedures. In addition, the new managers enable staff to make their own contributions and, in doing so, to generate greater identification with, and commitment to, the corporate success of the organization. As part of this, great value is placed on the establishment and dissemination of appropriate organizational cultures, thus encouraging shared values to socialize staff and bind the organization together (Wood 1989). These principles are drawn from a wider shift in management paradigms during the 1980s which extended way beyond the public sector (represented, for example, in the work of Peters and Waterman

1982; Kanter 1984, 1989; Peters 1988). The new public sector managerialism draws on these notions of generic management, applicable beyond
the narrow confines of a single bureaucracy, and in doing so, stresses personal qualities and competencies above knowledge of specific rules or
bureaucratic procedures (Halford and Savage 1995; du Gay 1996b).

Osbourne and Gaebler (1992) combine the features of structural
change, outlined above, with the new managerialism pervading the
public sector in their notion of 'entrepreneurial governance'. Though
referring to the public sector in the USA, it is worth quoting them at
length:

> entrepreneurial governments promote *competition* between service
> providers. They *empower* citizens by pushing control out of the
> bureaucracy into the community. They measure the performance of
> their agencies, focusing not on inputs but *outcomes*. They are driven
> by their goals – their *missions* – not by their rules and regulations.
> They redefine their clients as *customers* and offer them choices –
> between schools, between training programmes, between housing
> options. They *prevent* problems before they emerge, rather than
> simply offering services afterwards. They put their energies into *earn-
> ing* money, not simply spending it. They *decentralize* authority,
> embracing participatory management. They prefer *market* mechan-
> isms to bureaucratic mechanisms.
>
> (Osbourne and Gaebler 1992: 19–20, emphasis in original)

As Clarke *et al.* (1994) point out, this new managerialism has not totally
replaced more traditional, neo-Taylorist forms of management with a
longer history in the public sector. Both these management paradigms
are active within the public sector today. Precisely how they interact and,
more importantly for us here, how different forms of managerialism and
manager articulate with professionalism and professionals should not be
a foregone conclusion.

Explanations for change

The sheer scale as well as the specific nature of change in the organization of the public sector raises a number of important questions for us.
Why have such dramatic changes taken place from the mid-1980s
onwards? Why has restructuring in the public sector taken this particular
form and direction? Specifically, why has recent change in the public
sector been so intimately tied together with critiques of professionalism
and the emergence of a new form of managerialism? A range of explanations for these changes have been offered, varying both in focus and in
level of analysis. In what follows we offer a brief overview of these explanations, concentrating in each case on the specific issues which they raise
about professional–managerial relations.

The New Right and the New Left

The first pair of explanations concerns the party politics of both Right and Left. On the one hand, an obvious explanation for change lies with the policies of successive Conservative governments with an ideological commitment to transforming the public sector. During the 1980s and 1990s, these governments aimed to cut public spending, to promote new forms of provision and to encourage business rhetoric as well as the actual involvement of private firms in the public arena (Cochrane 1993). Indeed, in part the government's reforms of the past 15 years can be understood as a 'cultural crusade' (du Gay 1996b: 151) to construct Britain as an enterprise culture. Through policies which emphasized a belief in individualism rather than collectivism, in markets as the most efficient distributor of resources and in reducing dependence on welfare state provision, New Right policies have promoted managerialism in the public sector and conceptualized this as part of a broader strategy to deal with (what they believed to be) Britain's pervasive and persistent economic problems (Farnham and Horton 1996). Imposing new managerial structures and endorsing new managerialist discourse became core strategies through which Conservative governments have attempted to turn ideology into practice.

On the other hand, an alternative explanation offered for recent changes in the public sector refers to political pressures for change from quite a different direction. During the 1980s, many urban local authorities were controlled by 'New Left' Labour groups and these were active in promoting considerable changes to the management and structure of local services (Gyford 1985). Linked to the New Left's roots in community politics, decentralization initiatives were particularly popular as a means of bringing services closer to the users and making them more responsive to their needs (Hoggett and Hambleton 1987; Elcock 1991). Connected to this, as new managerialist discourses spread through local government, local government staff themselves have taken the initiative in promoting customer care initiatives and a 'public service orientation' (Passmore 1990). These pressures have been particularly evident in local government, although parallels existed elsewhere in the public sector. For example, similar processes of resource and geographical decentralization were evident in the NHS (Exworthy 1994). Likewise, *Health for All* initiatives actively encouraged community participation during the 1980s (Ashton and Seymour 1991).

Both New Right and New Left pressures for change implied the shake-up of old managerial and professional privileges. The details of how this might happen were less clear. Should professionals be expected to change? Should managers be encouraged to control professionals more effectively? Could processes of change be the same across different professions and in different parts of the public sector? Translating these political arguments into practice could, in principle, establish a number of different scenarios implicating professionals and managers in quite different ways.

Breakdown of consensus around the welfare state

Moving away from the micro-level specifics of party politics, it has been argued that these can only be understood in the context of a wider crisis in the welfare state, indeed a wider crisis in global capitalism (Jessop 1991b). At the meso-level, it has been suggested that Conservative policies of the 1980s and 1990s were the outcome of a breakdown of consensus around the welfare state which had existed in the immediate post-war period of welfare settlement (Johnson 1987). While it is becoming increasingly clear that popularly held assumptions of such consensus are inaccurate (Glennerster 1995; Mohan 1995), political divisions over the organization and funding of the public sector certainly became more obvious during the 1970s. Principles which had, for a while, seemed universal – such as the inevitable expansion of the welfare state (understood as the only realistic way to meet public demand) led by professionals (understood as the only group able to determine appropriate forms and levels of provision) – were increasingly challenged: the Labour and Conservative parties came to adopt clearly different positions.

This widened the options for new forms of organization, new principles and new practices within the welfare state. As the old certainties were challenged, established relations between professionals and managers necessarily became the subject of scrutiny.

Structural crisis

More fundamentally still, it has been suggested that beneath these political divisions lie structural conditions which will inevitably lead to a crisis in the welfare state. Marxist-influenced commentators point first to the nature of the state within capitalist society and, second, to the nature of capitalism itself in order to explain recent developments within the welfare state. Here the state's role is understood as caught between two contradictory imperatives: namely, to promote capital accumulation and, at the same time, to redress the inimical effects of capitalism (O'Connor 1973; Gough 1982). State institutions become *both* a burden on the economy (an obstacle to capitalist development) *and* a political and social stabilizer (necessary to continued capitalist development) (Offe 1984). It is in relation to this stabilizing (or legitimating) function that the activities of professionals and public sector managers become important. Offe (1984) suggests that 'process' mechanisms provide one of the key means through which the state's legitimating function is fulfilled. Here he is referring to the definitional and decision-making procedures within state bureaucracies which act to screen certain activities or groups from state assistance. The state legitimates certain professions (for example medicine); in return, professional practices and ideologies are seen as modes of social control or regulation working in the long-term interests of capitalism (see Jones in this volume). Similarly, public sector managers are used to rationalize state imperatives in bureaucratic (therefore 'non-political' and publicly acceptable) terms (Harrison 1988; see also Harrison in this volume).

Within these structural accounts capitalism is conceptualized as a *dynamic* process. In particular, commentators point to the *inherently* cyclical, boom–bust, nature of capitalist economies. The knock-on consequence of cyclical crises is a fiscal crisis in the welfare state. Put simply, as workers' earnings slump, demand for state services increases yet, at the same time, the state is less able to meet demands because taxation income is falling. Precisely these conditions might be said to have prevailed in Britain from the mid-1970s onwards. In this context, the state still has to fulfil its contradictory role of support for and legitimation of capitalism but, clearly, new ways have to be found to achieve this compromise. It is here that the emergence of new forms of managerialism – with all the implications we have already seen for the content and organization of professional work – becomes important. Specifically, the shift from a needs-led, professionally determined model of welfare provision to a market-led, managerialist model might be seen as one means through which a new legitimation of capitalism, rooted in the conditions of 1980s and 1990s, has been achieved.

Building on these accounts, it is sometimes suggested that we are in the midst of a shift from a 'Fordist' regime of capitalist accumulation to a 'post-Fordist' regime. In this formulation, Fordism is marked by mass production and mass consumption, linked together by the nation-state which guarantees the provision of standardized services to the masses and ensures a welfare safety-net of universal goods and services. As Fordism faltered in the face of global economic competition, capitalism evolved a new regime of capital accumulation (Hoggett 1994), and post-Fordism emerged in which both production and consumption became increasingly fragmented, divisions in society multiplied (for example, along lines of ethnicity and sex as well as Fordist class divisions) and the nature of the (welfare) state became characterized by 'post-bureaucratic control' (Hoggett 1991). In linking post-Fordism with this new form of organizational control, Hoggett (1991) argues that traditional forms of bureaucratic management were adequate only so long as the public sector was operating under conditions of stable, mass production and consumption which allowed standardization of services: i.e. Fordism. In the 'permanent innovation economy' (Hoggett 1991) (i.e. post-Fordism), state organizations must become more responsive, dynamic and innovative. Decentralization and marketization are two key and interrelated ways to achieve this.

Decentralization marks a shift away from the Weberian/modernist ideal form of bureaucratic organization, characterized by set rules and procedures within strict lines of control and authority extending upwards through a pyramid hierarchy. While the Weberian ideal was dominated by principles of centralization and formalization (Hoggett 1991), post-bureaucratic control replaces hierarchies with decentralized authority and an emphasis on outcomes rather than rules, on results not methods (Hoggett 1991). Decentralization also serves as a prerequisite for the introduction of market relations. Once discrete, semi-autonomous units are established, specific budgets can be attached and units can be instructed to carry out their own buying and selling of goods and services. Within this system, control comes to depend on *contractual* relations, rather than traditional bureaucratic authority.

On the one hand, then, the attack on bureaucracy embedded within this account can be interpreted as an attack on (old) managerialism. On the other hand, decentralization involving the devolution of both managers and managerialism can be interpreted as a threat to the autonomy of professionals at the lower levels of welfare state organizations. Certainly, decentralization places managers and professionals in closer contact, removing the 'safety zone' of hierarchical distance in more traditional bureaucracies (Exworthy 1992). Precise outcomes will depend, however, on the degree of marketization, decentralization and the responses of both professionals and managers, collectively and individually.

Questions

Whether we focus on the New Left, the New Right, longer-term developments in post-war British politics or more structural changes to the global economy it is clear that, *at all levels* of analysis, the process underlying change in the public sector has fundamental implications for professional–managerial relations, both now and in the future. A central theme embedded in all the above accounts concerns the organization and delivery of public services: who manages the public sector? From this several related issues arise, concerning the principles by which services are managed, the authority and responsibility of those managing, and the methods of evaluating those services. The ramifications of such issues for relations between professionals and managers are many and manifold. How have existing arrangements for managing and delivering services been affected? Have the roles of existing managers, bureau-professionals and professionals changed? How have interactions between managers and professionals been shaped? We outline these empirical questions and associated theoretical questions in greater detail in the following sections.

Management and professions: interactions across the public sector

Thus far we have sketched our terrain in terms of the emergence across the public sector of a new managerialism which has potentially profound implications for professionals in particular but also for 'traditional' managers. While professional groups have, of course, always taken independent action to change their own internal practices, the *initiative* over the past decade clearly lies with the new managerialism and the challenges it poses. We have been careful, however, not to imply that the outcome of such challenges is already known or, indeed, readily predictable. This unwillingness to offer simple predictions may seem surprising. After all, if we accept much of the mainstream research on managers and professionals, which assumes that managers and professionals are clearly distinct and inevitably in opposition to one another, the battle lines seem to be drawn clearly enough (although we still cannot say who will win). We prefer to pose this scenario of unresolved conflict as just one possibility. Certainly, examples can be found of managers and professionals at loggerheads, in conflict over power, status and authority as well as over convictions about how organizations or services should be run. Given recent changes, we might expect *conflict* between professionals and bureau-professionals on the one hand and managers on the other for several reasons. Some professionals may have personal fears about the fate of their careers, about being sidelined into 'practitioner niches' (Crompton and Sanderson 1990) where they are limited to practising as professionals while others take the more senior managerial roles. Similarly, some professionals may have concerns about their ability to perform in the new entrepreneurial culture (Scase and Goffee 1989). More generally, doubt may be expressed over the ability of new forms/structures of management to deliver public services effectively, and specifically, about the applicability and transferability of managerial techniques formulated in private sector to public sector management (Newman and Clarke 1994). Further, some argue that the ethic of public service depends on standardized bureaucratic procedures and unquestionable professional expertise which may, in fact, be fatally undermined by the new managerialism (Newman and Clarke 1994; du Gay 1996b).

Notwithstanding the potential for conflict, we also have reason to think that other outcomes may also result from the introduction of the new managerialist agenda. As indicated earlier, in most parts of the public sector, professionals have always taken on some managerial tasks. Not least, to do so has marked progression up the career ladder for many professionals. It may well be that professionals will adapt to incorporate new managerial skills into their repertoires as part of a career strategy. The new managerialism is not solely an external imposition on professionals. Further, for some, certain values and principles implicit in managerialist discourses have broader appeal. For example, among those professionals involved in the new urban Left alliances of the early- to mid-1980s, principles of consumer care and strategic management were popular and pre-dated central government policies of marketization or general management (Gyford 1985). The new managerialism is not simply about controlling professionals, but may also herald new patterns of compromise or collaboration between managerialism and professionalism (Harrison and Pollitt 1994). A striking example of this may be the conversion of professionals into managers. This may be particularly obvious as individuals' careers progress, but since the decentralization of management responsibilities down the hierarchy is a key aspect of the new managerialism such patterns of compromise or collaboration may become more pervasive still. For Hoggett (1991, 1994), this trend is the distinctive feature of contemporary change: 'rather than attempt to strengthen "management" in order to control "professionals" the strategy shifts towards creating managers out of professionals . . . A new generation of unit managers begins to emerge who combine technical expertise with managerial competence' (1991: 254).

More generally, du Gay (1996a) has suggested that recent reforms in the public sector are turning all staff into 'entrepreneurs', thereby endorsing entrepreneurial values in their work activities and, indeed, across the different spheres of their lives. Arguably, this kind of outcome constitutes a more effective form of control than is possible where there is explicit conflict. If professionals and bureau-professionals come to evaluate their own objectives and performances through the criteria of marketization and/or entrepreneurial values, this is surely more effective than the external imposition of such criteria and conflict over their appropriateness (Miller 1992). In this way it may become difficult to distinguish whether it is managers who are imposing their agenda on hapless professionals or whether professionals are strategically embracing managerialism which they perceive to be in their best interest. Most likely both processes are taking place. While this may still leave questions about the degree of 'choice' in such instances, the general point – that managerial–professional interactions in the new climate are not necessarily conflictual – remains.

The major empirical theme addressed in this book concerns relations between professionals and managers across the different parts of the public sector. Our initial question is an apparently simple one. What is the nature of professional–managerial interaction in the public sector in the specific context of the new managerialism? In this collection, we bring together studies of three different professions – medicine, social work and teaching – in three different parts of the public sector – local government, the NHS and state education. Combined, these three subsectors account for a large proportion of all public sector spending. In each case there is clear evidence of new forms of managerialism and changing managerial–professional dynamics. At the same time, some *distinctions* between the three sectors are immediately apparent. In particular the detailed structure of each sub-sector varies; the timing and particularly the degree of change varies from one sector to another; and finally, the history and status of each of the dominant professions in each case is markedly different. Our comparative approach allows us to explore further our initial contention about the uneven constitution of managerial–professional relations across the public sector and to pursue a number of complex questions about management, about professions and about their interrelations. In both cases we can explore the significance of differences between sectors and between professions.

The chapters collected here pose a range of questions within this broad framework and offer some provisional answers. However, interactions between managers and professionals – even in the particular context of the new managerialist public sector in Britain during the 1990s – are not finished or fixed but are dynamic and on-going. From this a number of more general theoretical questions arise, of importance beyond the specific confines of current circumstances in the public sector.

Theorizing management and professions

The empirical questions which we are asking about management, professions and managerial–professional interactions in the public sector also raise some broader theoretical questions. Arising from our discussion so far, our initial question concerns the *constancy* of the categories 'managerialism' and 'professionalism'. Certainly much of the literature on managers and professionals has attempted to ascribe fixed and clear meanings to these terms. One of the most recent examples of this is found in Savage *et al.* (1992), who suggest that the main difference lies in their respective and distinctive cognitive, or knowledge, bases. Savage *et al.* argue that professionals are dependent on 'cultural assets' derived from education and embodied in specialist knowledge of a given area of practice. By contrast, Savage *et al.* argue, managers are dependent on 'organizational assets' derived from practical organizational experience and from their position in the organizational hierarchy. These assets are not transferable because they are specific to that organization. Thus, while the terminology of 'assets' is new, the account by Savage *et al.* endorses many of the key points made in the literature on managers and professionals more generally.

But how far do these distinctions describe professionals and managers in the public sector today? Do 'cultural' assets and 'organizational' assets still clearly distinguish professionals from managers? Looking at professionals in particular, how are individuals and professional bodies responding to the new managerialist climate generally and to new managerialist interventions more specifically? Does their future lie in strengthening their distinctiveness and unique skills by enhancing their cultural assets? Or does the emphasis on managerialism in today's public sector encourage the inclusion of organizational assets into the repertoire of professional skills and competencies?

Turning to managers, does the new public sector emphasis on managerialism encourage the enhancement of the organizational base to their assets? Or does the *new* managerialism require something different? In short, we are asking whether the basis of distinction between professionals and managers (in the public sector at least) is shifting as a consequence of public sector restructuring specifically and changing notions of what represents 'good' professionalism and 'good' managerialism more generally.

In his debate about definitions of 'professionalism', Freidson (1994) argues that to seek a fixed position is futile: professionalism has always been a changing historical concept, rather than a generic one. While recent changes in the public sector mark a period of particularly rapid change (at least for the professionals employed there), perhaps the spread of an entrepreneurial culture reaches beyond the public sector, denoting change for all professionals. If this is the case, it is important to place these considerations in the context of other debates about the changing nature of professionalism. Three main schools of thought have emerged from this debate (Freidson 1994). First, there have been long-running suggestions that deprofessionalization is taking place (Haug 1973; Starr 1982). In this scenario, professionals are losing their cultural authority in terms of prestige and trust. This is largely thought to be due to broad social changes including consumerism, increased general levels of education (thereby reducing the gap in knowledge between professionals and lay people), public concern with the privileges accorded to professionals (pay, status, etc.) and the expansion of expert computer systems (effecting the 'rationalization and codification of expert knowledge' – Elston 1991: 64). Second, there is the proletarianization thesis, which suggests that professional labour is being transformed as it becomes increasingly dependent on employment in bureaucracies (Oppenheimer 1973), thereby losing its independence and becoming subject to the rule of managers like any other occupational group. Both theses suffer from a lack of specificity in terms of process and consequence (Elston 1991), and hence they fail to convince writers such as Freidson (1994). Friedson offers his own, third, school of thought, suggesting that the future for professionals may be one of internal combustion. As professions begin to fragment internally due to the increased bureaucratization of professional associations (as part of a move towards more credible self-regulation) and with greater specialization within individual professions (especially the increasing separation of administrators from rank-and-file practitioners), Freidson suggests that the coherence holding a given profession together may be undermined or even disappear as members cease to share the same interests. This trend, Freidson claims, may pose the more insidious threat to the future of the professions.

Evaluation of this scenario depends partly on the outcome of our earlier questions about assets. Specifically, are professional groups taking on organizational assets and in doing so redefining the nature of 'professionalism'? But even if we discover that this is indeed the case, the core of Friedson's argument requires us to examine how evenly or homogeneously organizational assets are being acquired by professionals. The internal combustion thesis suggests more than a redefinition of what 'professionalism' is, but a fragmentation within professional groups previously understood to be united. Such analyses will help to determine whether we are witnessing a major transformation in managerial–professional relations or simply yet another apparently imminent end to professionalism, which never quite materializes.

Overview

The chapters collected here offer a range of perspectives on both the empirical and the theoretical questions posed above. They not only focus on different parts of the public sector, they also adopt different analytical and theoretical tools, focus on different aspects of the debate presented in this chapter and therefore make their own arguments.

In Chapter 2, Rob Flynn maintains that throughout the recent period of public sector restructuring, essential differences between management and professions remain. Flynn argues that these differences are rooted in the distinctive values and practices of management and professions respectively. Further, he argues, there is a persistent social need to place trust in bodies of professional expertise which bestows on professions an 'irreducible' core of autonomy (p. 34) from managerial control. Thus, Flynn claims, fundamental and irresolvable differences remain between managerialism and professionalism which the present climate of change will not alter. Indeed, with tighter control of public spending, the conflict between managers and professionals may only be further exacerbated by arguments over resource allocation.

In Chapter 3, Chris Jones builds on Flynn's abstract analysis by contextualizing the debate in a history of social work professionalization. While Jones takes a neo-Marxist perspective, in contrast to Flynn's Weberian approach, their arguments are remarkably similar. Like Flynn, Jones maintains that a core difference in overarching values lies at the heart of inherent conflict between management and social work. Unlike Flynn, however, Jones concludes that social workers are losing the battle with the new managerialism to such a degree that something approaching a takeover is happening. While the difference in values marks the distinctiveness of social work professionals at an abstract level, in practice social workers are compromising their professional identities by taking on management roles and responsibilities.

In Chapter 4 Stephen Harrison also provides evidence that a merging of professional and managerial roles is taking place, this time in medicine.

However, contrary to Jones's analysis of social work, Harrison does not see these developments in medicine as a 'takeover' as such. Rather, clinical autonomy and medical identity remain strong. Indeed, Harrison argues, the maintenance of clinical autonomy can be understood as central to the success of the new managerialist agenda in health care. This paradox emerges as doctors take on managerial responsibilities, specifically budgeting, but implement these within a framework of clinical autonomy. In this way (professional) legitimacy is bestowed on financial (managerial) decisions about health care rationing. Put bluntly, in the face of likely public hostility, the doctors can get away with rationing more credibly than general managers ever could.

In Chapter 5 Ian Menter and Yolande Muschamp offer more evidence that professional and managerial roles are merging, this time in education. Through a variety of institutional reforms, the redistribution of managerial responsibilities to school level has changed teachers' work roles and career routes. Head teachers have taken on an almost entirely managerial role, while the work of classroom teachers is increasingly shaped by managerially led concerns. However, while a merging of managerial and professional roles may be taking place in the daily workload of teachers, Menter and Muschamp show that this is not an easy compromise for individual teachers to make.

In Chapter 6, Gordon Causer and Mark Exworthy review evidence across medicine, nursing, teaching and social work. While they point out that there has always been some blurring of managerial and professional roles in the public sector, they argue that this has become far more pronounced in recent times. Indeed, Causer and Exworthy claim, the categories of 'manager' and 'professional' now no longer encapsulate the range of positions which have emerged between the two.

Finally, in Chapter 7, Susan Halford and Pauline Leonard consider how interactions between notions of 'managerialism' and 'professionalism' might impact at the level of individual identities. Using secondary accounts of recent changes in education, and more general research on managers across a range of sectors, Halford and Leonard reject suggestions that new managerialist discourses simply 'take over' the identities of public sector professionals. Instead, drawing on post-structuralist debates about identity, they argue that the outcomes are highly complex and unstable.

Note

1 Examples include local government reorganizations in 1972, 1986 and 1996; NHS reorganizations in 1974, 1982, 1991 and December 1997; educational reforms in 1986 and 1988.

2 | Managerialism, professionalism and quasi-markets

| Rob Flynn

Introduction

The social sciences have a crucial role in informing arguments about public policy, and the relation between professionals and managers in the public sector is a longstanding source of controversy. There are important empirical as well as normative questions – do professionals exercise too much power? Should professionals be made more accountable to managers? Whose interests and objectives do each of these groups serve? Would citizens or consumers be better served if there was less, or more, professional control of services? Could the application of managerial techniques (such as total quality management, for example) improve the way services are delivered by professionals?

While recognizing that no single discipline can claim to give comprehensive answers to such questions, it is none the less true that sociology has provided wide-ranging and useful analyses of bureaucracy and professionalization. In the literature, those analyses have focused on three interrelated issues: the nature of expert knowledge and occupational autonomy, the effects of managers' and professionals' actions on clients, and the degree to which these groups are accountable and can be regulated. This chapter does not examine those issues in particular, but instead tries to develop four contemporary arguments which flow from them. First, although we should be cautious about using grossly simplified concepts of 'management' and 'professions', there are fundamentally important contradictions between their values and practices, and this may potentially result in conflicts between them. Second, the emergence of the so-called 'New Public Management' does not remove the ultimate source of tension in the public sector – control over resource allocation decisions. Third, the recent development of 'quasi-markets' within the welfare state (and moves towards privatization) will have mixed and contradictory effects across different policy sectors, with varying consequences for managerial and professional relations. Finally, there are intrinsically problematic areas of social life in which risk and trust are embedded, and this necessarily entails dependence on experts' discretionary judgement which cannot be completely controlled by external agencies.

Before exploring these arguments, we must briefly refer to their context – in particular the crisis of the welfare state, and the apparent emergence of so-called 'post-Fordist' welfare systems – which are discussed in more detail in Chapter 1.

The context of change in public sector professions: the critique of welfare and 'post-Fordist' developments

Concern about the growing power of bureaucracy and professional groups is not a recent phenomenon. Much of the most important writing within sociology stems from Weber's and Durkheim's awareness of their significance. In the last 50 years, in addition to charting the emergence and impact of law and medicine, sociologists have also explored the rise of scientists and engineers, and turned their attention to the evolution of new kinds of specialist occupations – accountancy, industrial management, teaching, social work, etc. Then, as now, there was much dispute about whether the growth of professions reflected the dominance of a new type of scientific rationality and the promise of altruism and progress, or whether, far from being neutral or apolitical forces, such groups sought privileges and monopoly power to the detriment of their clientele, and served elite political interests.

Fundamental questions about whether we can trust professionals to be altruistic and competent, and whether they serve collective goals adequately and efficiently, have preoccupied writers from very different theoretical frameworks. Such questions have become more urgent in recent arguments about the role of the welfare state. It is significant that both the New Right and the New Left targeted modern welfare state professionals, albeit for different reasons. For those on the New Right (especially the 'public choice' school), state intervention was criticized for undermining economic efficiency and investment, as well as debilitating the enterprise culture through promoting welfare dependency. Professional groups were seen as self-serving producer monopolies whose influence on the economy and society was negative. The New Left also vilified professionals for exploiting clients in private markets, and accused professions in the paternalistic welfare state of disempowering citizens while facilitating bourgeois domination and social control (see King 1987; Barry 1990; Dunleavy 1991).

These approaches converged during the late 1970s with a common recognition that there was an endemic fiscal crisis in the modern welfare state, where demands for public services outstripped the capacity to generate tax revenues to finance those services; but there were divergent solutions for public policy. Writers from the New Right stressed the problem of 'ungovernability' and prescribed free market reforms, whereas neo-Marxist theorists such as Habermas and Offe recognized a *systemic* crisis in the rationality of advanced capitalism and stressed the inherent contradictoriness of welfare state policies (see Offe 1984; Taylor-Gooby 1991). Lash and Urry (1987), following Offe, suggested that we had entered a new era of 'disorganized capitalism' in which the Fordist system of mass production and consumption had become fractured and displaced. They argued that economic trends towards flexible work organization were paralleled by cultural, social and political transformations in which traditional class boundaries and identities were being eroded. They also noted that in this context, the professional and managerial groups (sometimes termed the 'service class') occupied a strategic position.

As Chapter 1 indicates, more recently there has been a vigorous debate about the extent to which these changes are concomitant processes in the evolution of a new type of 'post-Fordist' regime in the economy and society. Essentially it is argued that the post-war 'Fordist' mass production system (based on large-scale integrated firms, Keynesian demand management and a corporatist welfare state) was undermined by technological innovation, global shifts in the economy, and declining rates of economic growth. A new 'regime of accumulation' emerged in which new service industries displaced manufacturing, gigantic corporations dismantled their own hierarchical structures, the labour process and the labour market were forced to become 'flexible', and new highly differentiated consumption markets developed (see Jessop 1991a, 1994).

It is further argued that either as a direct result of these macroeconomic changes, or at least in parallel with them, the form and content of social policy was transformed, and a restructured 'post-Fordist' welfare state evolved. In this new kind of welfare state, there were said to be very similar processes of decentralization and flexibility (Hoggett 1990) and a shift away from universalist forms of collective provision towards more marketized, residual and variegated services, delivered through a mixture of agencies (Jessop 1991b). Probably the most important structural manifestation of this is the creation of 'quasi-markets' to stimulate purchaser–provider competition in the production and delivery of a wide range of social policies. The impact of quasi-markets is addressed in more detail below, but it is especially important to acknowledge its significance in the transformation of managerial–professional relations in the public sector.

Evidently there are many empirical and theoretical questions about whether a 'post-Fordist' explanation is convincing. There are important criticisms of its over-abstraction, implicit determinism and functionalism (see Loader and Burrows 1994). However, its heuristic value lies in its ability to relate internal organizational changes in the allocation of, and access to, welfare services to wider economic and political restructuring.

Thus for example Hoggett (1987, 1991) has persuasively argued that especially in British local government, a movement towards administrative decentralization and managerial devolution coincided with a reinforcement of centralized budgetary and strategic control. He further argued that part of the process of moving away from bureaucratic control – in which there were chronic problems with both professionals' and administrative discretion – was the development of internal decentralization (or greater organizational delegation) and external decentralization (i.e. tendering and contracting out). Following Hoggett, it can be seen that the problem of 'post-bureaucratic' control was dealt with by operational disaggregation and financial reconcentration. Consequently, as Hoggett has more recently observed (1994: 43), 'rather than try and control professionals by managers, you convert professionals into managers (i.e. by giving them budgets or setting them adrift as quasi-autonomous business units)'.

Thus the debate about a post-Fordist welfare state is relevant to understanding the contemporary context of managerialism and professionalism, and for concentrating attention on the apparent dissolution of established structures and practices. Flexibilization and fragmentation are leading to constant questioning of the roles of, and boundaries between, managers and professionals in the public sector precisely because 'the public sector' is itself being redefined and recomposed. However, while post-Fordist accounts provide general overviews of structural changes – and what Hoggett terms the 'technology of control' – little is said about the objectives and values of those engaged in the new public management. It is not at all clear what the new public service managers' (or professionals') goals are, but this has become a vital concern in a climate of competition and consumerism created by quasi-markets, as we shall further observe below. Before we can proceed to that discussion, it is necessary to review other key arguments about the nature of professionalism and managerialism.

Professionalism

There is a vast sociological literature about the concept of profession, and numerous studies of professionalization as a social process. Alternative approaches correspond to particular theoretical positions derived mainly from functionalism, symbolic interactionism and Marxism. Among these main approaches, the central questions and principal disagreements have been about:

• whether there are discrete and identifiable features of professions which make them different from other occupations, and whether there is a hierarchy of occupations in terms of their professional standing;

- whether it is necessary to challenge professionals' claims to expertise as ideological, and regard their activities as part of a wider process of social closure based on exclusion, to secure resources, status and power;
- whether it is mistaken to exaggerate the significance of professional autonomy, given that all occupations compete and struggle for control over the work process;
- and whether it should be recognized that organizational imperatives towards bureaucratization and routinization lead to a 'proletarianization' of professionals.

(For further discussion see, among others, Abbott 1988; Crompton 1990; Freidson 1986, 1994; Larson 1990; Murphy 1990; Witz 1992; Macdonald 1995).

Here the view taken is that a neo-Weberian account of social closure is most useful in explaining why certain occupations are more successful than others in claiming 'professional' expertise and why some have achieved state licence and mandate to control their own labour process. Social closure refers to the capacity for, and strategies of, social groups to exclude, or usurp, other groups in a struggle for control of scarce resources, valued social locations, and their associated privileges and status (see Parry and Parry 1977; but for critiques of neo-Weberian approaches, see Johnson 1995; Saks 1995).

However, it is also necessary to recognize (as Johnson 1972, and Fielding and Portwood 1980 argued) that the capacity for welfare state occupations to determine the content of their own practice, and the terms and conditions under which they work, is highly circumscribed in the public sector. There is in practice a constant dialectic between autonomy and heteronomy, between independence and subordination: as professional occupations seek to maintain their own control over the execution of tasks and self-regulation, other external bodies attempt to exercise increasing control over their training and performance. Consequently, in different policy sectors, and at different times depending on prevailing economic and political conditions, professions will encounter more or less stringent regimes of regulation.

Simple dichotomies of *either* professional autonomy *or* bureaucratic-managerial control are thus inadequate to describe the complex and dynamic relations which typify professionalized occupations. Neither absolute proletarianization nor professional dominance are likely to succeed, because experts will constantly seek markets for their skills and endeavour to maximize their independence; but at the same time employers (and representatives of clients) will continue to attempt to regulate and control expert labour. 'Autonomy' can be conceptualized at different levels of analysis – for example institutional autonomy refers to the jurisdiction claimed by a professional occupation and the extent to which it can secure legitimacy and state approval, whereas technical or work autonomy refers to efforts to determine terms, conditions and working practices, as well as the division of labour vis-à-vis other groups. Professional autonomy is thus contested, variable and contingent on many factors.

Within most organizations there are often struggles for power between different work groups or coalitions, as well as between superordinates and subordinates, for strategic control over policy and resources. Such struggles frequently reflect a basic tension within all divisions of labour, between what Fox (1974) termed 'high discretion' and 'low discretion' work. But as Freidson (1986, 1995) has emphasized, professional work is *inherently* discretionary, and its very indeterminacy places constraints on the capacity for external inspection and supervision. Nevertheless, this tendency towards the autonomous use of discretion (in its various forms) is governed ultimately by resource constraints. Freidson correctly points out that professional technical autonomy can only be exercised if resources are available, so the crucial issue is whether professionals can determine resource allocation and control resource use or whether distinctive managerial groups have encroached and consolidated control in this domain.

Managerialism

Management and managerialism have stimulated intense argument and large literatures in economics, industrial relations, organization and management studies as well as sociology and political science. It is difficult and dangerous to generalize from such diverse fields, but it is essential to focus on some defined features of managerialism as a set of beliefs and practices, and on management as a distinctive social group. Some of the most important questions to concern us are: What is management for? What are its goals and values? Does it constitute a countervailing social force in opposition to professionalism? Can management be compatible with the organization and delivery of *professional* services?

Management as a separate function within the work process emerged with the development of mass production in industrial capitalism (Clegg and Dunkerley 1980). It is inextricably connected with the development of bureaucracy and indeed derives its importance from the need for strategic planning, coordination and control of large complex decision-making processes (Dandeker 1990). In modern capitalist enterprises, maximizing profits (or output or productivity) for owners and shareholders necessitated an exploitative division of labour in which subordinate workers were expected to comply with superordinates' demands and instructions. It also led to the belief that industrial and other work organizations could be more efficient if responsibility for policy and planning and overall control was separated from implementation, routine operations and production tasks. Cadres of specialist managers and systems of surveillance and control were thus established to monitor work flow and quality, and to discipline the workforce, while other functions were also created (finance, marketing, corporate management) to plan investment and to assist companies with strategic intelligence about their products, customers and competitors. It is this cluster of activities and occupations we now label 'management'.

Reed (1989) has noted that management has been studied as a system of authority, as a set of skills, and as a social class or sectional interest group. He suggested a generic and apparently neutral working definition in which management is a set of activities and mechanisms for assembling and regulating productive activity (Reed 1989: ix). But like Clegg and Dunkerley, he also reminds us that management and managers assert the right to determine resource allocation, to resolve conflict within an organization and to impose ultimate authority by virtue of their role and delegated mandate from owners/shareholders.

The long-running dispute about whether business corporation managers are integral members of the capitalist class or relatively autonomous of capitalist interests is not one which can be appropriately discussed in this chapter. This aspect of managerialism concerns the 'ownership/control debate' about whether managers' objectives are identical, complementary or conflicting with capitalist owners (see for example Salaman 1982; Scott 1985, 1991; Edgell 1993). But it is important to note that the issues raised by that debate are relevant in the examination of current reforms in the public sector, since they concern the vexed question of managers' values and interests. In the public sector, the question of owners and shareholders is not directly comparable (since the state is the collective owner of public assets and resources) and it is commonly assumed that most managers and staff share similar (and until the advent of quasi-markets, non-profit) objectives in pursuit of the public interest. In legal terms, public sector managers derive their legitimacy and purpose from legislation and government policy, and are accountable bureaucratically to higher level officials and politicians. However, in the new quasi-market system with multiple purchasers and providers in competition, public accountability has become more opaque, and it is unclear whose goals and interests will shape the behaviour of local managers.

The important point, nevertheless, is that whatever their ultimate goals, managers in both private and public sector organizations have a primary orientation to *corporate* success, and endorse strategies which they themselves are instrumental in defining. Managers routinely exercise prerogatives of supervision and control over subordinates, and usually subscribe to the discourses of efficiency and enterprise. Their primary objectives are to ensure organizational survival (and usually growth) and their basic allegiance is to the company or organization. There are, of course, disagreements about whether variations in types of management practice correspond to macro-changes in the political economy and industrial structure – the most recent debate concerns differences between Fordist/Taylorist 'scientific management' and post-Fordist human relations and upskilling within flexible firms (see Chapter 1, and Bagguley 1991; Jessop 1991b; Clarke *et al.* 1994; Du Gay 1994). But the crucial point remains that managers assert the right to manage subordinates in those organizations in which they have executive authority, whatever methods are adopted. Management, whether in the public or private sector, is an authority relation and embodiment of organizational power.

Nevertheless we should not exaggerate the extent of managers' power – subordinates may challenge and evade managerial direction, and despite the apparent weakening of workplace trades unionism, employees of all kinds may explore various means of resisting managerial control. Even the most Foucauldian analysis must acknowledge that disciplinary power in modern corporations is contested (Deetz 1992). And as Reed (1993) implied in his account of postmodernism in organization theory, deterministic and mechanistic models of surveillance and control should be rejected in favour of more complex relations of agency and structure.

Professionals versus managers?

Such a contingent approach is necessary in analysing how professionals (expert labour) can be integrated into complex organizations in which hierarchical authority may be vested in non-professional managers. It is argued here that there are many latent structural and attitudinal contradictions between managerialism and professionalism, as Table 2.1 illustrates in ideal-typical form.

Table 2.1   Ideal-type contradictions

	Managerialism	*Professionalism*
Source of legitimacy	hierarchical authority	expertise
Goals/objectives	efficiency/profit maximization	effectiveness/technical competence
Mode of control	rules/compliance	trust/dependency
Clients	corporate	individuals
Reference group	bureaucratic superiors	professional peers
Regulation	hierarchical	collegial/self-regulation

Professionals justify their claims to autonomy and status in terms of their expert knowledge and skills, geared to effective performance of specialized tasks usually linked with individuals' problems. Their actions are based on a trust relationship with clients, and are subject to the approval, inspection and regulation by other professional peers. In contrast, managers *qua* managers claim their privileges on the basis of institutionalized hierarchical authority; their primary objectives are organizational efficiency (usually measured in terms of profit or surplus); and they require other staff to comply with organizational rules and their managerial commands. They are the agents or servants of corporate bodies rather than individual clients, and they are only accountable to, and subject to, evaluation by bureaucratic superordinates.

While it is recognized that a rigid dichotomy of bureaucracy versus professions may not operate in situations where many organizations are staffed by professional *employees*, and where some professionals themselves may be line managers, it remains the case that there are potential conflicts of objectives, values, reference groups and modes of occupational control. The extent to which such possible tensions emerge and influence policy and practice is likely to vary between types of profession and types of agency or service. As Freidson (1994) has cogently observed, the mere fact of employment by large organizations does not in itself threaten professionalism: the key issue is the concrete internal policies which control and limit professionals. The most significant elements in such control, as we shall see again below, are power over the allocation of resources; defining the obligations professionals have to their employing organization and their clients; the system for evaluating the standards of professional work; and methods of supervising professional work. It is precisely these elements which have come under scrutiny and reform in the evolution of public sector quasi-markets. We therefore need to examine the particular position of welfare state managers and professions.

Managers and professionals in the public sector

There have been longstanding debates within political science and public administration about who runs government, national and local – elected politicians or appointed officials? There is particular uncertainty about public sector managers' and professionals' accountability and decision-making power. Many writers, from different political standpoints, have challenged the apparently inexorable expansion of influence by non-elected officials in a wide range of public policy areas. There have been criticisms of bureaucratic rigidities and departmentalism, professional incompetence and malpractice, and paternalistic attitudes towards clients, which were argued to be pervasive in the welfare state (see Wilding 1982). Some sociologists also argued that local state officials were increasingly important 'independent variables' in the creation of new types of social inequality based on access to collective consumption and welfare services, constituting a form of 'urban managerialism' (Pahl *et al.* 1983; Saunders 1986). Such theoretical critiques have recently been matched by a series of structural changes and reforms.

In brief, during the 1980s, central government initiated a series of measures to control public expenditure and to redesign the civil service and local government, emphasizing the virtues of the 'three Es' – economy, efficiency and effectiveness. In doing so, it challenged many taken-for-granted assumptions about the working practices and organization of traditional public administration. However, despite these attempts by central government to weaken local government and rein-in public professionals – which involved a massive restructuring of the public sector, and creating an entirely new set of institutions for governance (quasi-markets and quangos) – it is still acknowledged that the position of professionals remains problematic (see Dunleavy 1982; Pollitt 1984; Stoker 1989).

As Chapter 1 has indicated, throughout the 1980s numerous managerial reforms were introduced. In the civil service the 'Financial Management Initiative' had an enormous impact, requiring all departments to set up procedures for better corporate management and performance measurement. The 'Next Steps' devolved operational functions to executive agencies, separated from strategic policy (see Gray and Jenkins 1994). In the NHS, general management was established in 1983, which, in combination with various other organizational changes, had profound consequences, weakening the autonomy of medical and nursing professionals (see Harrison *et al.* 1990; Flynn 1992; Harrison 1994b). In local government, much tighter controls on spending were enforced and councils' monopoly position as suppliers of some services was undermined by compulsory competitive tendering and contracting out. In health, education and personal social services, the establishment of internal markets, with 'competition' between agencies newly constituted into 'purchasers' and providers', was geared to a complete transformation in the 'culture' of the public sector. Cost efficiency, consumer responsiveness and supplier competition were core objectives in this process, and these all necessitated the subjugation of professionals to managerial authority (see Flynn 1990; Pollitt 1990; Cutler and Waine 1994; Taylor-Gooby and Lawson 1994).

As Pollitt (1990) and others argued, this new generic managerialism embodies a number of different assumptions and values which are assumed to be unproblematic. These include the idea of progress through greater economic productivity, technological innovation, worker compliance and managers' freedom to manage. It is a diffuse ideology which privileges commercial models of organization and management practice, and insists that these can (and must) be transplanted to public sector services. It presumes management to be both a technical matter and to be inherently virtuous. But as Gray and Jenkins (1994) also observe, although managerialism pretends to be neutral and value-free, this ideological claim is coming under increasing challenge, not just from political responses by citizens but also from attempts to (re)define public management theory.

During the late 1970s and 1980s a new school of thought, and a new set of remedies, called 'The New Public Management' (NPM, sometimes also called the 'public service orientation') appeared, promising the prospect of a fusion of 'best practice' in the private and public sectors (see Clarke *et al.* 1994). According to Hood (1991, 1995a, 1995b) this is an international trend in public administration, as governments in different countries attempt to slow down the expansion of public spending and stimulate private market forms of provision in formerly public services. Its essential components include: more active and accountable management; explicit standards, targets and measures for performance; a stress on results, quality and outcomes; the break-up of large units into smaller decentralized agencies; more competition and a contract culture; more flexibility in the terms and conditions of employment; increased managerial control over the workforce and efficiency in resource allocation.

Hood (1995a, 1995b) argues that while the principal goals of NPM are cost cutting and doing more for less, there is little empirical evidence that increases in outputs and most importantly *qualitative* improvements are actually achieved, or have been attributed to the implementation of NPM alone. Moreover, as Pollitt (1990) and Gray and Jenkins (1994) have stressed, while no one could object to NPM's insistence on more efficient use of resources and greater responsiveness to consumers, this sidesteps the questions of efficient for whom, and accountable to whom. It also ignores the question of whether efficiency or consumer responsiveness are to be the only – or the dominant – values and goals in the public sector. It fails to recognize the fundamental difference in the forms of accountability entailed by, and the differences between, consumers in a private market exchange and citizens with social and political rights. Indeed, ends and means are often confused in the managerialist ideology, and political choices are obscured in managerial jargon. Is efficiency the ultimate *objective* of public policy, or is it rather a prerequisite for the means to attain that objective? Most importantly, the new public management says very little about resource allocation and rationing, and their distributional effects – the fundamental parameters for all decision-making. The emphasis on cost-effectiveness alone does not solve the permanent dilemmas of arbitrating between numerous and conflicting demands.

These questions of goals and values and accountability are thus unavoidable in deciding whether public management can usefully borrow and adapt private sector models. They are also important in understanding the implications of quasi-market competition in the public sector, to which we can now turn.

Quasi-markets

The 1980s Thatcherite project of rolling back the state encountered substantial practical problems (for example the growth of social security expenditure to finance unemployment) and political opposition (for example public anxiety and protests about 'cuts' in the National Health

Service) so that wholesale privatization of welfare and public services was abandoned in favour of more pragmatic reforms. These entailed the imposition of provider competition through internal markets – public financing and state ownership remained, but public services had to respond to consumer demand and could no longer monopolize provision. The defining features of quasi-markets were that provider agencies were ostensibly non-profit, were tax-funded, and though users did not pay for services directly with cash, suppliers' revenue depended on consumer demand rather than bureaucratic allocation (Le Grand 1990). It was assumed that consumers would experience more choice and better value-for-money and providers would be forced to improve efficiency and quality, spurred by the threat of competition.

Observers acknowledged that there were serious difficulties with information, of risks of opportunistic behaviour and adverse selection, and possible threats to equity. Variations in the *type* of service or policy sector were also seen as important, with housing and education approximating the requirements for quasi-market structure, social care in an intermediate position, and health furthest away from market conditions (see Bartlett and Le Grand 1993; Le Grand and Bartlett 1993).

Evidence about the impact of quasi-markets has only begun to emerge recently, and it has been (not surprisingly) mixed. In the NHS for example, in relation to criteria of quality, efficiency, choice, responsiveness and equity, there is no consensus on whether quality has been improved solely because of the internal market; efficiency gains have been observed but cannot be directly attributed to the reforms alone; evidence indicates only very little increase in choice and responsiveness to patients; and there are signs of a two-tier service and further inequities (Le Grand 1994).

A review of findings in several policy areas indicates several continuing problems. First, there are doubts about whether market structures can develop, because of information asymmetry (where consumers lack knowledge of services and cannot exercise real choice); barriers to entry (where alternative suppliers find it difficult to enter the market); and lack of information on outcomes (where it is difficult to evaluate quality of provision). Second, the current contracting system favours cream-skimming (that is, providers have incentives to select the most valuable or least costly clients) or cost reduction rather than service improvement. Third, there are still doubts about the degree to which providers are accountable to users, especially since direct representation of consumers or electoral influence by citizens does not exist or has been removed (Propper *et al.* 1994).

In the non-acute sector of the National Health Service, for example, Flynn *et al.* have argued that there are inherent problems with, and significant limitations on, the quasi-market and contracting system for primary and community health services (see Flynn *et al.* 1995, 1996). Many key aspects of community health services cannot be codified into meaningful categories for contracting, outcome indicators are intrinsically problematic, and there are large components of this work which require substantial professional discretion which is threatened by purchasers' determination to negotiate tightly specified contracts and greater efficiency.

Disappointingly, across the different policy sectors there is as yet little empirical information about the motives and objectives of provider agencies and their interaction with the system of regulation in a managed market (Bartlett *et al.* 1994). Birchall *et al.*'s (1995) study of NHS Trusts, grant-maintained schools, and 'large scale voluntary transfer' housing associations found that managers believed recent reforms had given them more autonomy, but this varied by type of service. At the same time there was evidence of increased centralized control over these agencies, a shrinkage of *professionals'* work autonomy and corresponding expansion in the power of line managers. In a longitudinal survey of public and private sector managers, Poole *et al.* (1995) found that the enterprise culture and market values had permeated into the public sector, but there were also some continuities in the 'public service ethos'. Thus while over 90 per cent of public sector managers believed that consumers' interests should be paramount, those managers were less hostile to trades unions than private sector managers. Similarly, while 68 per cent of public managers regarded their own role as 'professional', they reported a deterioration in their own job satisfaction and an awareness that increased organizational controls (increased regulation and surveillance) were at odds with their own expectations about greater managerial autonomy promised by the enterprise culture.

It is here that we return to the problem of the relationship between managerialism and professionalism. In a wholly private market, solo professionals or partnership firms charge clients fees for service and are subject to legal and professional regulation. While it would be naive to idealize their altruism and duty to clients (Saks 1995), it remains true nevertheless that private sector *professionals'* livelihoods are entirely dependent on their responsiveness to clients and the maintenance of trust. Broadly, what distinguishes their position is their ability to determine their own conditions of labour, their level and terms of remuneration and the content of their practice. By contrast, in the public sector and especially in the quasi-market, professionals' abilities to set their own pay, terms and conditions of employment, and to control task performance, are largely constrained, or strongly influenced, by governmental regulation and increasingly by managerial authority.

As Table 2.1 suggests, private and public professionals' claims to authority derive from expertise and skills, their practice is governed by external or collegial regulation (peer review), and they assert that their primary concern is the interest of individual clients. Increasingly the ability of public sector professionals to realize these aspirations has been attenuated, as managers stress organizational imperatives in a

competitive market. Unlike professionals, line managers have no immediate responsibility for individual clients (except for certain cases of
social work), but rather for the overall efficiency of their organization,
and they are ultimately accountable to higher level executives and local
or national politicians. It therefore remains an open question as to
whether intermediate and senior managers pursue objectives which are
wholly compatible with and supportive of those pursued by 'front-line'
professionals. Equally, it is uncertain whether such front-line professionals' objectives are always congruent with the corporate goals of their
employing agency. An additional question in the quasi-market contract
culture – suffused by 'Citizen's Charters' and consumerist rhetoric – is
whether *managers* can legitimately claim that they also represent consumers' interests indirectly, through delegated authority from politicians, and by virtue of a duty to implement quality assurance systems.
These questions are currently being answered through the uneven development of quasi-markets, which contain within them two probable
scenarios.

The first trajectory involves a systematic managerial strategy to depro-
fessionalize expert labour, to proletarianize it – subject it to increased
fragmentation and de-skilling, more bureaucratic monitoring and performance evaluation. There is already some evidence of such a trend in
education, health and personal social services (Cutler and Waine 1994).
Lloyd and Seifert's (1995) study of four NHS hospitals indicated that
although recent management responses to financial deficits were
unplanned and short-term, Trusts now face pressure continually to drive
down costs in order to secure contracts and to meet efficiency targets.
Regrading of jobs (varying, usually lowering, the 'skill-mix' of staff),
short-term contracts, local pay bargaining and performance-related pay,
together with contracting out work and competitive tendering exercises,
are all devices which have been used and are likely to be practised more
frequently in quasi-market conditions. Hitherto they have been mainly
applied to low paid and 'ancillary' staff, and non-core services, but
increasing competition between providers must inevitably lead to their
extension to other staff and core functions. If a regime of cost control is
followed by even more stringent and explicit rationing, as Norman Flynn
(1994) has argued is likely, then there will be more managerial control
over workers, more detailed monitoring, and more individualized evaluation of performance.

The other likely scenario entails a complex form of marketization in
which there is uneven 'reprofessionalization'. Here it is conceivable that
in certain areas and for certain groups of services, some former public
sector professionals will transfer to wholly private practice and encourage people to exit from state-financed provision (for example, in primary
health care, 'total fundholding' is a very short step away from the American model of a 'health maintenance organization'). At the same time,
within the public sector some 'entrepreneurial' professionals (and

managers) might form coalitions with 'privileged' consumers (inevitably involving 'cream skimming' and preferential selection), and attempt to secure disproportionate shares of state funding. In the meantime, other less favoured areas and more stigmatized clients, and less competitive professionals, will receive fewer resources and these residualized clients will experience deteriorating conditions and poorer services.

The latter scenario of course, refers to the possibility of some successful 'opted out' (grant-maintained) schools, hospital Trusts, GP fundholders and housing associations securing a market niche and flourishing, while others become insolvent and close. The adherents of quasi-markets may argue that this end-state will not occur, first because contestability will force those with poor performance or falling standards to improve, and second because more efficient suppliers will take over those providers and turn them around.

There are political and practical difficulties with this because of the large sunk costs in capital and equipment – can existing infrastructure be abandoned and new buildings, etc. be constructed rapidly to meet changing demand? Is it feasible (not least in terms of accessibility) for clients to transfer to alternative providers? Will the basic assumption of a universal welfare system with equal social and spatial access be overturned? If a quasi-market really depends on competition, the reality of winners and losers has to be credible, and market failures must occur. If there is quasi-competition, then there must be increased variation in the range, type and quality of services provided: such differentiation may entail fragmentation, residualization of some groups and some types of service, and the weakening of universalism (Flynn 1997).

Conceivably, both scenarios might occur at the same time. Taylor-Gooby and Lawson (1994) note signs of increased divisions between front-line workers and managers; and in addition to growing inequalities between 'mass' and 'minority' services, they anticipate greater fragment-ation and inequity of provision. Newman and Clarke (1994) also argue that the public sector displays contradictory elements of both 'neo-Taylorist' and 'new wave' management, the former stressing efficiency and more-for-less, the latter extolling consumerism and quality.

However, whether deprofessionalization or uneven reprofessional-ization occur, the objectives and criteria for resource allocation and rationing remain crucial, and disputes over values – efficiency versus equity, universal versus selective services, citizenship rights and needs versus consumer demand and preferences – far-reaching. When there is sustained pressure on providers to compete and to maximize revenue, either scenario is possible, but in each case it is unclear whose interests will be paramount in selecting a strategy for resource allocation and in determining priorities, and whether managers and professionals will have common or divergent objectives.

As Taylor-Gooby (1994) astutely observed, the postmodernist rhetoric of choice and diversity dismisses concern for universal welfare values while obscuring the fundamental oppressions of inequality. There is a very real possibility that professionals in the public sector, in an era of quasi-markets, may be forced to forgo their assumed commitment to service according to need *as professionally defined*, and orient their activities to those aspects of their work which are *managerially defined* as being most cost-effective or revenue-maximizing. The pressures, and opportunities, to do this will vary between services because of their different market structures, and because of their varying social significance and political salience. There is also likely to be variation within and between professional, and perhaps among managerial groups. There may be tensions, for example, even within agencies, between corporate finance directors and business managers and service or unit managers. There may also be divisions between front-line professionals and those professionals charged with monitoring quality and carrying out service audits.

In quasi-markets, therefore, the axis of potential conflict is not simply between managers and professionals, because within both purchasers and providers different interests will struggle for control to define the organizational 'mission' and to invoke a consumer mandate. It is also probable that purchaser agencies, claiming to represent the wider public interest, and wishing to negotiate value-for-money contracts and enforce regulation, will define much more precisely the parameters within which provider professionals and managers must operate. But providers currently have the monopoly of direct access to and interaction with their clients through service delivery. Provider managers and professionals may claim greater knowledge of local needs and priorities, have more reliable information, and control the necessary skills and technology. Thus the quasi-market institutionalizes a tension between purchasers and providers which will have varying effects in different services.

Where purchaser agencies attempt to exert more control over providers' expenditure and the content and quality of services through budget negotiations and contract specifications, it can be expected that provider managers will – even if they contest such moves – be constrained to comply, and will in turn endeavour to exercise even more control over their own professional staff especially in relation to priority-setting and the volume and throughput of work. In cases where provider agencies can reduce their dependency on single large purchasers, or diversify into surplus-generating (and fee-paying) services by exploiting their market advantages, then they may have more agency autonomy. However, paradoxically, this in itself may not necessarily reduce the scope for managerial influence over professionals. Debates over business strategy and extended controls over the labour process may be equally contentious in an ostensibly entrepreneurial and expanding provider. The issue again is the extent to which professional skills and expertise are marketable, and whether, or how far, professionals' work autonomy and discretion are to be trusted by managers.

Conclusions: discretion, trust and uncertainty

Giddens (1991a) has argued that the importance of abstract systems and expert labour is so deeply embedded within modern societies that it is taken for granted. Abstract systems comprise those institutionalized sets of relations and forms of rational knowledge that transcend particular groups and individuals and are capable of being implemented across time and space, providing both structural context and mechanisms for action. They include, for example judicial systems (legal codes), monetary systems (international banking and credit), scientific and technological systems (air traffic control; medical techniques, etc.). Expert knowledge consists of the particular competencies, specialized knowledge and practices used by occupations claiming autonomy and authority to solve specific types of problem, and is usually based in abstract systems. Although these may be taken for granted, that does not diminish their significance, however.

Giddens (1991a) among others has stressed the institutionalized power of surveillance, and the contingency of risk and trust, in what he terms 'high modernity'. He argues that our dependency on expert systems (highly complex, esoteric but systematic bodies of knowledge, skills and practices) extends beyond the scientific and technological domain to all aspects of social life, and their opacity renders the issue of trust highly problematic. He further argued (Giddens 1991b), that no one can now opt out of modern expert knowledge or abstract systems, so risk and trust are intertwined and expressed in a form of 'blind faith' – that is, confidence in the correctness of principles and practices that one cannot fully know or understand.

Of course this is the intrinsic problem of professionalism – can professionals be trusted to perform competently, and how can their behaviour be regulated so that it benefits clients? Ultimately, professionals assert the authority of expertise and claim disinterested integrity. Their ability to sustain these claims rests on the indeterminacy of the knowledge and skills that they possess, and the necessarily *discretionary* content of their work. Their knowledge and skills may be codified and systematized but they cannot be completely programmed; outcomes of intervention are to varying degrees uncertain, and the particularity of individual cases and clients requires professional discretion, in both senses. It is precisely the exercise of professional judgement – rather than the application of a bureaucratic rule – in the process of providing a service which constitutes what Rueschemeyer (1983: 48) called 'the irreducible core of autonomy'. Moreover, Ray and Reed (1994) have argued that in a 'post-bureaucratic' world characterized by constant economic restructuring, information technology expansion, and cultural hyper-differentiation, 'expert work' and specialized knowledge cannot be effectively contained within a model of bureaucratic control.

However, Lipsky (1976, 1991) noted that the administration and delivery of social welfare policy is inherently discretionary, but for this very reason careful thought must be given to the limits of this discretion and to the mechanisms for its control. The major unresolved issue consists of the amount and form of regulation to be applied to professional practice, and whether managers are appropriate and legitimate as regulators. It is feasible to create systems in which professionals are their own managers – indeed this is the intention and effect of many of the quasi-market reforms. But as the discussion above and elsewhere in this volume suggests, there are fundamental contradictions between the logics and rationalities of managerialism and professionalism which will create new conflicts and problems.

The increased use of contracts intensifies such tensions. The contract culture has exacerbated a tendency towards greater formalization and has intensified managerial moves to control the workforce, although the overall impact is not yet certain (Walsh 1995). If – as Walsh suggested – there is a prospect of conflict between more market-oriented strategies and traditional public service objectives, then the issue of managerial control of professional discretion is not only an internal organizational matter but a trend having important consequences for social policy and political debate about the public sector.

Some commentators have warned of a future situation in which there is concurrently both an 'anarchic' welfare state (in which there is confusion about the boundaries between – and the operating rules of – the 'public' and 'private' sectors) and a 'gridlocked contract state' (which becomes excessively juridified – Hood 1995a). Others have predicted a quasi-market of more explicit rationing, price competition and managerial retrenchment of services, in which service quality and user influence are of minimal concern (Flynn 1994).

In all cases the project of 'managerialization' is not just 'incomplete' (Clarke *et al.* 1994) but never-ending, as it inevitably seeks to control – or co-opt – professional autonomy. The perennial problem is that professionalized service delivery entails priority-setting, rationing and the allocation and use of resources. Professionals are likely to insist on exercising and retaining the prerogatives of 'discretion', 'judgement' and expert knowledge to justify their decisions. Managers, by contrast (including those who are themselves also professionals) are likely to seek means of closing off those indeterminate and open-ended features of professional practice, in order to conform with broader corporate goals and resource constraints. The relationship between these two different groups and different sets of objectives and values, centres on the contested nature of trust in fields in which the outcomes of intervention are uncertain.

To conclude, it can be acknowledged that as a possible solution to the managerialism–professionalism dilemma, and in contrast to the rationalities of the market and bureaucratic hierarchy, 'networks' and 'clan'-based forms of trust may offer alternative and more effective modes of organization for the production and delivery of complex services (see

Thompson *et al.* 1991; Flynn *et al.* 1996). If network organizations and clan-based trust were to occur on a large scale, then the latent contradictions between managers and professionals might not become manifest, or could be accommodated more pragmatically.

However, such network systems depend entirely on the acceptance of high discretion/high trust relationships and an endorsement of reciprocity and collaborative interdependence rather than adversarial and competitive exchanges (Fox 1974). In Britain, quasi-markets as they have evolved to date do not appear to support such a development and may indeed be detrimental to it. Other limited and partial solutions to the problem of trust and control include more sophisticated and extended systems of professional accountability to clients – through audit and quality assurance procedures. However, while there are some indications that these systems and procedures are gradually becoming more widespread, there seems to be very little explicit debate about *managerial* accountability to citizens/clients, or about the criteria and values underlying managerial policies. While it is perfectly reasonable to accept that managers can challenge professionals to account for their decisions and practices, it is also necessary that managers' own objectives should be scrutinized and be open to challenge. Whether the current experiment with quasi-markets will facilitate any of these developments remains uncertain.

3 | Social work: regulation and managerialism

Chris Jones

Introduction

The emergence of managerial control within British state social work is a relatively recent phenomenon. Until the late 1970s there is little reference to managers and managerialism in the social work literature. That is not to say that there was no concern about the regulation or control of social workers before this time. Rather, the preferred form of control was professional self-regulation in which social work education was the key site. However, within a relatively short time span between the mid-1970s and the late 1980s there was a series of dramatic changes in which the earlier confidence in professional social work education as the key regulatory process appeared to evaporate, and managerialism came to the fore. This chapter sets out to explore this process of transformation and the more general question of the regulation of social workers.

Unlike many other key areas of social policy, social work is a relative newcomer within the state's panoply of welfare activity. Thus although it has a long history – in the voluntary and quasi-state sector – social work only established itself as a major state welfare activity with the acceptance of the Seebohm Report in 1968 and the subsequent creation of the local authority social services departments in the early 1970s. Until that time, social work at least as a state sponsored activity was a rather marginal activity, fragmented across a range of central and local government departments, and struggling for legitimacy and acceptance (Jones 1983). Even after the government's adoption of the Seebohm recommendations there were still those critics who felt that social work should not become the 'fifth' social service (Townsend *et al.* 1970) and that the needs of clients would be better met by improvements to the social security system and commitment to full employment rather than by employing more social workers and creating new large social work departments.

Social work's struggle for legitimacy and its subsequent 'lateness' in achieving its objectives, when compared to other key welfare occupations and agencies, have been decisive influences in shaping British social work. It has, for example, been one of the more turbulent areas of state welfare, with endless professional boundary disputes as it has struggled to establish its own discrete section of the state welfare domain. From the late 1940s onwards, state social work has not enjoyed any sustained period free from significant legislative change. The tempo might have increased since 1979, but for nearly 50 years state social work has been subject to rapid and significant change. Such factors have shaped a particular trajectory of occupational development and regulation when compared to other areas of public policy. Hence this chapter takes a brief look at the context and nature of British social work in order to provide a more adequate understanding of its current regulation and control. Without such context-setting it is simply not possible to grasp the significance of the changes that have taken place and the manner in which over a relatively short period of time state social work has been transformed from a self-regulating professional activity into a managed and increasingly externally regulated set of tasks.

The social work process and the need for education

Social work poses a number of potential challenges for a class-divided and polarized society. Unlike many other key social policy practices, such as education and health provision, it is class-specific. It not only operates almost exclusively within the working class, but its main efforts have always been directed at the most impoverished, vulnerable, and from the perspective of the state, the most troublesome of its citizens (Schorr 1992). Moreover, unlike the police or the prison service that operates over a similar terrain, social work does not approach its client population simply from the perspective of controlling or punishing the dangerous classes. From 1945 onwards, social work has claimed state sponsorship and funding on the grounds of offering control through treatment and rehabilitation rather than just containment and surveillance. This rehabilitative imperative has been central to the expansion and development of state social work in Britain (Jones 1983). It was precisely on these grounds that social work claimed legitimacy and governmental support. It promised to ease the costs of delinquency, crime and welfare dependence by claiming an expertise to resolve expensive and recurring social problems through casework methods undertaken by skilled social workers. However, it is also an approach which is potentially problematic for the state in that social workers could, on the basis of their close involvement with some of the most disadvantaged, reveal not so much the problems of their clients but the deficiencies of a society and the manner in which it persistently and systematically reproduces disadvantage. This capacity of social work to reveal the bleak side of a society that is among the richest on earth and which claims to be humane and civilized should on no account be underestimated. The necessity to ensure that social workers do not cause embarrassment by exposing the realities of the societal underbelly remains one of the driving forces in the regulatory development of the occupation and is a core factor in the emergence of macho managerialism during the late 1980s.

The argument that a wide range of social problems could be 'cured' by methods which demanded gentle and persuasive intervention in the lives of families and individuals who were commonly and widely stigmatized and demonized, historically situated social work in a somewhat precarious position both within the state and in the wider society. It is after all an approach that contradicts a variety of state practices and policies that have traditionally considered substantial elements of social work's client population as the undeserving poor, the residuum, the dregs of society who should be punished, constrained and, if possible, eradicated. Periodically reinforced over time by notions derived from eugenics and the persistence since the latter part of the nineteenth century of social Darwinism, the plight of many clients has been commonly constructed as an accurate reflection of their lack of worth: They were where they were because of their lack of capacity and moral worth. Inevitably, social work's stance of salvation with respect to this much maligned segment of the population has contributed to its rather contested status and to it becoming a rather easy target for the Right, including some of the more reactionary elements of the tabloid press (Franklin 1989).

While social work throughout its history, and certainly since 1979, has attracted criticism for being 'soft' with its clients, the reality is inevitably more complex and paradoxical. The compassion of social work as an institution of welfare has always been conditional. A measure of that conditionality can be gauged by the widespread distrust of social work and social workers in many working-class neighbourhoods, where it is viewed as an agency to be avoided. Moreover, unlike so many other areas of state welfare provision, social work's development has been almost exclusively driven from on top. It has never been the subject of working-class or popular demands. That is not to deny that social work has not in some significant ways marked new departures in state activity towards some of the most impoverished and disadvantaged. The emergence after the Second World War of an invigorated social work profession built around Freudian perspectives and methods does mark a distinct break with the brutalism and cruelty of earlier state practices. Resonating with the social democratic temper of the period, psycho-analytically informed social work exemplified a phase of optimistic welfare offering rehabilitation and social inclusion to those who had previously been seen as unhelpable and thereby deserving of policies of studied neglect or containment as epitomized by the Poor Law.

But the compassion and liberalism of social work were both conditional and specific, referring principally to a method and practice; they did not derive, for example, from an interpretation that clients' problems were connected to and caused by systemic processes inherent in the operation of capitalist societies. Thus clients were still held to blame – the most usual attribution was the failures of mothers to socialize and care for their children – for their plight. What was taken as compassion was the insistence of social work leaders that the possibility of changing clients' character depended upon the establishment of a personal and trusting relationship between the client and the social worker. The pioneering figures of social work, such as Octavia Hill (see Garrett 1949: 220), were well aware that without some outward sign of acceptance and sympathy on the part of the social worker it would be impossible for them to achieve their goals of remoralization. After all, social work is concerned with bringing about change in the way clients live and behave. If this is to be permanent and self-regulated then it is deemed to demand 'internal' changes in values and perspective. Hence, great stress has been placed on the personal qualities of social workers.

The succession of government reports which led to the expansion of state social work after the Second World War were insistent that great care should be given to personal suitability in the selection and recruitment of students to social work courses (Curtis Committee 1946: Appendix 1; Mackintosh Report 1951: 38; Underwood Report 1955: 20). Although professional social work courses today continue to recognize the importance of personal qualities of candidates, it no longer dominates the selection process as once it did. Prior to 1970, it was not unusual for social work to use psychiatrists in the selection process, and there were many tutors who concurred with Penley's view of candidates that:

> Academic proficiency was not needed, but the right kind of personality emphatically was. The prospective student ought to have at least the beginnings of a thought-out philosophy, her personality should not be aggressive and good manners were most desirable.
>
> (Penley 1946: 267)

This emphasis given to selection and identifying those with the 'right' personal qualities for social work reveals a longstanding concern within social work about the myriad dangers that confront a welfare strategy based on sending 'nice' and 'caring' people into the midst of society's most disadvantaged and vulnerable. Given the individualized and personal features of the social work process with clients – in which the relationship cannot be directly supervised and managed, thereby allowing the social worker considerable autonomy – it becomes vital to the very success of the activity that the social worker does 'the right thing'. In social work terms, this means working on the basis that the problems confronting clients (most commonly a family or household) are largely of their making and that the solutions to the problems are similarly to be found in changing their behaviour and outlook.

However, ensuring that social workers 'do the right thing' is not easily guaranteed, as social work leaders since the late nineteenth century have recognized. The difficulties are many, and the dangers considerable. One of the pioneering features of the Charity Organization Society (COS) was its early recognition that professional education could make a critical contribution to making social workers 'safe'. By the beginning of this century, a carefully constructed curriculum drawn selectively from the social sciences combined with practice supervision by a trusted 'elder' in charge of careful selection to ensure that only those with a predisposition to 'gradualism' were accepted. This was a fundamental truth of the COS and has remained largely intact until the beginning of the 1990s. This educational and training package, with its supervision of the student and the provision of legitimating 'scientific' knowledge, was considered to be essential to effective social work and was required by all those who were to have responsibility for social work provision. Moreover, the introduction of such formal courses in 1902, and the subsequent demands throughout the rest of the century to extend such provision to all those employed as social workers, was never simply about the training and education of social workers, important as this was; it was intended to establish social work as an activity that no longer could be considered the domain of well-meaning amateurs, or some natural expression of the obligation of the privileged to the impoverished.

It needs to be noted that it was not until the late 1970s that the majority of those employed as state social workers were professionally qualified, which meant that for much of the twentieth century, social work professional education was largely restricted to those who managed and supervised untrained colleagues. This enhanced the status of social work education for it was never just a passport into the occupation of social work but the gateway to the most influential positions in the emerging occupation. For these practitioners, given their occupational and professional status, it was especially important that they be made as safe as possible. This was not simply a matter of ensuring that they adopted a perspective that never fundamentally challenged the existing order, they also needed to be immunized against one of the most corrupting influences identified by successive generations of social work writers and educators, namely undisciplined sentimentality.

The social work literature from the late nineteenth century onwards through to the current period warns of the dangers of social workers being overwhelmed by the hardships and miseries confronting their clients. Without the protection of professional education, social workers have been considered easy prey to highly manipulative clients (who paradoxically are commonly presented as rather pathetic people until it comes to pulling the wool over the eyes of the naive social worker, when they become experts without equal). In addition, there is acknowledgement given to the sheer awfulness of the social conditions which are endured by so many clients. Both of these can undermine the resolve of the social worker to see the difficulties largely as the consequence of individual failings; they can certainly provoke spontaneous acts of generosity such as giving out cash or goods. Without proper assessment and supervision, such acts have long been held within social work as dangerous in that they undermine self-help and familial self-reliance and thereby encourage dependency. (Many social workers, as Pearson (1975) discovered, engaged in various kinds of occupational subterfuge to do what they could for clients, although since his research many agencies have introduced measures that seek to make such 'Robin Hood' activities more difficult.) Nevertheless, notwithstanding this occupational deviancy, even the most cursory reading of some of the key texts that have been used on social work courses over the past century reveals a most extraordinary tradition of condemnation and contempt for large segments of social work's client population. One of the main targets of this literature, the students on social work courses, are regaled with accounts which present clients as 'clamorous and greedy children who can never be satisfied' (Irvine 1954: 27), as people whose 'dependency is pervasive and the client sucks from neighbours, shopkeepers, bartenders and news vendors as well as family members and social workers' (Richan and Mendelsohn 1973: 15), and as people who deserve their poverty (Davis and Wainwright 1996). For all the language of compassion and empathy there is running alongside it another language of hate and contempt – a principal paradox of social work under capitalism.

For British social work then, professional courses were never simply about improving occupational standards or milestones on the way to gaining professional standing or status. They performed such functions but they were always more important than that. They were the key sites for the reproduction and regulation of a particular type of welfare intervention in the lives of the most impoverished and distressed. They were charged with the awesome responsibility of making what had the makings of a difficult activity under capitalism – a seemingly soft and compassionate response to those most stigmatized and excluded – safe and reliable. One aspect of this task is the immunization of the social workers themselves from 'contaminating thoughts and practices'. In a telling passage at the beginning of this century, Bannatyne wrote of social work education as providing social workers with

> the faith which never doubts that beneath the unequal, fettered, unloving and unlovely social conditions, as beneath the perplexed, half-sorrowful, half-hopeful religious questionings of today, there lies hidden a new heaven and a new earth . . . Only through such a faith can our self-control become strong enough to stand by and see suffering and misery go untouched by us, because no remedy we can as yet devise would relieve the individual sufferer except – we believe – at the cost of his own, or others' greater injury in the future. Only such a faith can make our self-control strong enough to resist the temptation of sacrificing moral and spiritual strength in others to

their physical comfort and ease – to refuse to believe that when for ourselves, we *know* our industry and independence, our self-respect and family responsibilities to be of greater value than any other material possession, the reverse can be true for the poor.

(Bannatyne 1902: 342–3, emphasis added)

And over 40 years later, we discover T.H. Marshall arguing in similar vein about the necessity and purpose of social work education as being to satisfy the personal needs of the social workers themselves, to prevent internal mental conflicts, and to answer questions which they are bound to ask and must be enabled to answer to their own satisfaction if they are to give themselves whole-heartedly to their work, inspired by a sense of purpose. In this connection I should like to refer once more to MacIver's book (*Contribution of Sociology to Social Work*, 1931). He points out the limitations of social work: the services offered are often only palliatives, leaving root causes unaffected. It may even be that they perpetuate the causes by making the effects more tolerable. Yet the social worker is moved by an emotional desire to help in the creation of a better world. How can this urge be reconciled with the limitations of the daily task? And he answers:

The social worker must in short be socially educated, must acquire as a student of economics and sociology a background of intellectual convictions. So fortified, he or she can advocate further goals while still doing a day's work . . . The social worker who has no background of social philosophy is at the mercy of a thousand discouragements.

(Marshall 1946: 16–17)

The end of fortification

The 1970s proved to be a decisive decade for state social work. Not only were social service departments created in England and Wales and social work departments in Scotland, there was also the subsequent expansion in the number of social workers and an even more stark rise in the demand for professionally qualified social workers. Between 1970 and 1975 the annual output from qualifying courses doubled from just under 1500 to over 3100 (*CCETSW* 1975). These developments alone meant that social work had to go beyond the narrow pool from which it had previously recruited, which in turn impacted on courses and their recruitment patterns. Furthermore, the reorganization entailed a root and branch transformation of social work agencies as previously discrete organizations became unified. These reforms transformed the organization of social work services.

For social workers this led to a profound shift in organizational culture as they moved from small agencies to larger departments (Glastonbury 1975). In addition, the creation of these departments saw the beginning of the end of social work's tradition of vocationalism. Reorganization brought about improvements in salaries and the possibility of career progression as a consequence of the creation of hierarchical systems and by being embedded in a local authority structure. Many of those who had benefited from the expansion of higher education, through the development of the polytechnics in the 1960s, now saw social work, for the first time, as a viable career option, one where their degrees in the social sciences might have some relevance.

These changes had a significant gender dimension. As state social work expanded and offered career and salary prospects comparable to other public sector occupations such as teaching and local government administration, so men increasingly came to dominate the upper reaches of the occupation. This was starkly revealed in the appointments to the newly created director posts consequent on reorganization. It was a process which virtually wiped out women from the senior management positions – in an occupation where the overwhelming majority of the staff and clients were women and which, along with nursing and primary school teaching, was held to be 'women's work'. In 1976, there were 95 male directors (91 per cent) as against 9 women (9 per cent) and 77 men as deputies (86 per cent) as against 13 women (14 per cent) (Davis and Brook 1985: 4). The reorganization of state social work not only generated new bureaucratic departments but marked a regendering of senior management. According to Foster's research (1987, 1988), men were much more career minded than women, with the men likely to 'department hop' in order to seek promotion whereas women were more likely to stay put and seek advancement through the same agency over a much longer time frame. Likewise, women in Foster's research were revealed as being more concerned with clients and their agency's development over time, whereas many of the men in senior positions were looking for the 'main chance'. As Lupton (1992: 99) noted, 'rather than the values of continuity of service and familiarity with the historical and local context of the department, the attributes being sought in the new managers appear to be: "youth, masculinity and mobility"'.

Just as significant were the changes in the nature of state social work provision itself which were consequent upon the reorganization of state social work agencies. Contrary to much of the rhetoric of Seebohm, the creation of unified departments with their single point of access did not so much benefit clients as it did other front-line state welfare authorities. Most referrals in any event did not come from clients themselves but from such official sources as social security offices, schools, courts, police, health agencies and the like. The creation of a unified department greatly improved this third-party access. As a result, the reorganization greatly accelerated the trend of social services departments to become not so much an equal front-line agency with its own agenda of preventive family casework at its core, but more a subordinate agency with a servicing and support function. The pace, nature and form of work became increasingly influenced by third-party state referrals; one consequence was that the focus of social work activity became increasingly determined by external agencies – such as debt collection and client supervision – rather than by the apparent needs of clients. This became an increasing feature of state social work during the 1980s as cutbacks in public spending and increasing levels of poverty and unemployment raised eligibility levels to front-line services. State social work services in this context came under increasing pressure as people found themselves ineligible for other welfare support (see for example Becker and Silburn 1990).

In the introduction, attention was drawn to the turbulent character of state social work. The 1970s was a most dramatic decade for social work. It opened with social work in triumph, with its long sought-for goals delivered by Seebohm and Kilbrandon and its treatment orientation confirmed by key legislation such as the 1969 Children and Young Persons Act. However, the decade ended with social work demoralized and confused, anxious about its future and in turmoil occasioned by a national social workers' strike in 1978/9. The strike exemplified the extraordinary speed and far-reaching nature of the changes to state social work over a very few years. In less than ten years large numbers of social workers had turned their backs on their newly formed professional organization (BASW) and joined trade unions. Many were now seeing themselves first and foremost as employees of the local authority and not as professional workers (Simpkin 1979; Bolger *et al.* 1981). In the context of social work these were dramatic changes.

The scale and scope of these changes in the organization of state social work during this decade led to decisive shifts in social work education and the beginning of a process of change which was to bring to an end the key role of professional social work education as the main site of occupational regulation and control. These functions and responsibilities began to pass increasingly to the managers in the state social services agencies.

As I have argued in detail elsewhere (Jones 1989, 1996b), there were a range of internal pressures in addition to those noted above which plunged social work education into crisis. Courses were not only having to manage an increased demand for qualified social workers as a result of Seebohm reforms (NALGO 1989), but they were also facing an increasingly querulous student body. The 'crisis' of social work education was principally about its perceived inability to control, regulate and appropriately socialize neophyte social workers – in other words, a failure in its core task. Courses were seen by many agency managers as no longer capable of making social workers safe, and in some cases, courses were accused of fermenting dissent and radicalism (Jones 1983).

Not immune to the critical temper of the period, social work tutors were confronting a more questioning student body who were not prepared to accept unconditionally the traditional assumptions of psychosocial casework and familialism. Developments in the sociology of

deviance, social policy, psychiatry and psychology, alongside the renais-
sance of feminism, the impact of the civil rights and black movements,
and gay and lesbian liberation activities, proved an explosive cocktail for
social work education. Its knowledge, skills and methods core was simply
insufficiently robust in the face of students' challenges; it was exposed as
being little more than a rather crude ideological edifice supporting a set
of questionable conservative assumptions about clients, poverty and
social injustice and the British social system as a whole (Cannan 1972;
Kendall 1972; Bailey and Brake 1975).

The social work academy had failed to meet these challenges and to
guarantee that its courses would produce students capable of working in
the new constrained and stressed environment of pressured social service
departments. This triggered a process whereby its previous position of
occupational dominance passed over to agency managers. The Central
Council for Education and Training in Social Work (CCETSW), created in
1972 to validate and monitor professional social work education, was one
of the key examples of this process of transformation (Webb 1996). Brewster (1992) – who had been a CCETSW officer – has traced the manner in
which CCETSW was transformed into an agency of new managerialism,
with the social work academy being virtually routed from the Council
over a period of 15 years, and agency managers taking their place.

The gradual accretion of power to state agency managers – with their
being given increasing control over the *entire* curriculum and not just the
placement – was first signalled by the creation of a new work-based professional qualification, Certificate of Social Service (CSS), in 1975. It was
later fully consolidated in the new single qualification (Diploma in Social
Work, DipSW) implemented in 1989 (Jones 1989). This process of change
is worthy of more detailed attention than can be given here, but one of
the themes running through the various changes made to social work
education was not only the transfer of power from the academy to the
state agency managers, but the manner in which the social science
knowledge base to the curriculum had been scrutinized and controlled.
The process of anti-intellectualization led to the increasing rejection and
marginalization of the traditional knowledge base of social work. For
much of social work's history the social sciences were pillaged to legitimate its practice and perspective. However, as the social work academy
could no longer modify the influence – particularly of the critical social
sciences – on the curriculum and on the students, this legitimating
knowledge became contaminating knowledge and had to be expunged.
In the process, the discourse of professional preparation for social work
changed from education to training, to the acquisition of skills and competencies rather than knowledge and understanding.

The New Right and social work

The impact of the New Right since 1979 has transformed social work practice, just as it has many other aspects of state welfare activity. Positive
welfare, with its rhetoric of treatment and inclusion, has lost its place as
the *raison d'être* of welfare, to be replaced by containment, rationing and
surveillance. In the specific case of state social work this has entailed the
activity becoming far more antagonistic to clients (see Jones and Novak
1993), and there has been a bombardment of legislation which has fundamentally changed the role and tasks of many social workers. In many
agencies social workers have been retitled as 'care managers' to indicate
that their focus is no longer on providing services to clients but rather on
the allocation and gatekeeping of resources.

Such important changes signify a fundamental shift of focus in British
state social work, in which the needs and demands of the agencies –
rather than those of the clients – are given primary consideration. In the
contemporary welfare system, state social work agencies do not require
highly informed or educated, research-aware social workers. These are
now regarded as positively unhelpful qualities that make for questioning
and criticism. Rather, what is now demanded is agency loyalty, an ability
to follow instructions, to complete procedures and assessments on time,
to modify and placate client demand, to manage inadequate budgets and
to work in such ways that will not expose the agency to public ridicule or
exposure (see Hadley and Clough 1996). This is the critical set of conditions which has heralded the onset of new managerialism in state social
work. Simply, the tasks expected of state social workers in the contemporary welfare system are such that professional self-regulation is hope-
lessly inadequate; what is required is a managed workforce with no
illusions about professional autonomy or ideals that service to the clients
is paramount. This in turn reveals the extent to which the New Right state
has not been particularly concerned to win over the minds of welfare professionals such as social workers, teachers, doctors or nurses, but has
instead been focused on ensuring the 'right' conduct on the job.

Professional social work education – for so long held to be the key to
the regulation and reproduction of the occupation – is consequently
becoming increasingly marginalized. Many state agencies are now developing NVQs for their front-line staff (Cannan 1994/5). These are
entirely consistent with the pro-training and anti-education approach to
staff development. Such courses also leave the agencies wholly in control
of the curriculum as well as keeping the students out of the potentially
contaminating environment of higher education. As state social work has
become more concerned with rationing and gatekeeping scarce resources
and the surveillance of clients (Parton 1991) so the need for professional
education will increasingly diminish. The most telling example to date
of this process is the case of the Probation Service: in 1996 the Home
Office decided to remove the requirement for newly appointed probation

officers to hold a professional social work qualification. This was regarded as a restrictive practice that prohibited the recruitment of newly redundant NCOs from the army. This type of person, with their background in military discipline (and presumably unencumbered with fancy sociological theories), was regarded by the government ministers as ideally suited for a probation service that was to be more focused around punishment and control rather than social work and treatment (Williams 1996). As the rehabilitative concerns of social work are pushed increasingly to the margins it is virtually certain that professional education is going to be limited to a small cadre of specialist child care and mental health workers. This minority of specialists will continue to require and expect a knowledge-based education, whereas it is probable that the majority of social services workers will, in the future, receive limited training opportunities determined and provided by their employers.

It is difficult to envisage how traditional professional social work education might have withstood the pressures of the Right's transformation of state welfare after 1979. That social work has survived at all is in no small part due to its quiescence in the face of this project and its preparedness to jettison its clients in order to secure its survival. The social work academy was no different from the rest of the occupation and sought survival through passivity in the hope that a low profile and not rocking the boat would keep their livelihoods intact.

In one of the few publications which has addressed these developments Holman (1993) berated social work, and social work leaders in particular. He contends that under the New Right there has been within social work a growing acceptance of poverty and inequality, with social work chief officers prepared to believe 'that gross inequality is acceptable' while accepting huge salaries. He further accuses these social work leaders of being motivated by the 'greed of personal gain' rather than by the professional ideals of service to the public. He also presents evidence to demonstrate that many chief officers have 'shown astonishing enthusiasm in embracing the Government's programme of minimising the local authority function, imposing a market culture and destroying direct provision of public services' (Holman 1993: 47).

Sadly, many of these developments in contemporary British social work have not been widely contested from within the occupation. Rather, there has been a pervading sense of resignation which has much to do with the social work occupation looking to the state for its legitimization. From the end of the Second World War in particular, British social work saw its future and well-being as linked into the state; until 1968 it battled and organized to gain state recognition and funding for its own discrete welfare agency. As the Fabians indicated at the time of the publication of the Seebohm Report (Townsend *et al.* 1970), the main beneficiaries of the report were not clients and the working class poor but the social work occupation. British social work in contrast to social work in some other places has a history of looking up to the state for its endorsement and legitimation. It has no record as an agency of reaching 'down' to its client base for support and meaning.

Those social workers who have had a different orientation, who have been genuinely moved by the plight of clients and the manner in which inequality and hardship are endlessly reproduced, have always been considered a problem and a threat. The social work establishment has been little different to the Colonial Office of old, with its anxieties over whether or not its chosen colonial servants would 'go native'. Consequently so much of mainstream social work has been historically constructed around two key concerns: one has been the regulation of social workers, preventing their contamination either by clients or from 'troubling thoughts', the other has been that of presenting the problems of poverty and inequality in a manner which constructs the clients as the problem. For all the rhetoric of compassion and care there have never been any substantial coalitions between clients and social work agencies or social work courses; this exemplifies the manner in which clients are so highly disregarded.

The results of this history and these traditions are all too evident today. Hadley and Clough's (1996) study of the community care reforms gives startling evidence of social workers' fear of senior management, as does the emergence of 'samizdat' newsletters in social service departments as social workers try to resist their managers' apparent desire to drive liberal social work out of their agencies. These cases are not simply the consequences of the new managerialism. They are the consequences of being in an occupation which as a whole has never taken its clients seriously and which consistently took the side of the strong against that of the weak.

4 | Clinical autonomy and health policy: past and futures

| Stephen Harrison

Introduction

The principle of clinical autonomy (the term 'clinical freedom' is used synonymously) has been pervasive in the organization and management of the UK National Health Service (NHS). A working definition of this principle is that a fully qualified specialist physician or general practitioner (GP) is entitled to diagnose, treat and refer his or her patients as he/she wishes, within the limits of self-perceived competence and of the physician's perception of patient need and (in practice) available resources. This is an elastic definition which essentially represents a claim both to be unmanaged themselves and to exercise some form of control over most other health care occupations (Freidson 1970), though commentators such as Tolliday (1978), Elston (1991) and Coburn (1992) have argued that these two matters should not be conflated; indeed, in the latter's view, 'dominance' (control of other occupations), 'autonomy' (freedom from control by other occupations) and 'subordination' (being controlled by another occupation) form a *continuum of control*. In the UK context, medical dominance has not usually extended to day-to-day supervision of other occupations, but has rather been exercised through involvement in their regulation (Larkin 1983) and through the ubiquity of the ideology of health and illness – this is conventionally shorthanded as 'the medical model': the view that ill-health equals individual pathology, and that medical interventions are individual ones.

It is the claim to autonomy, to be unmanaged, that forms the focus of this chapter. It is a claim that has been treated quite literally by physicians; it has, for instance, been extended to allow surgeons to perform procedures of which they have little, if any, experience (Buck *et al.* 1987), to determine their own arrangements for timing clinics, and to determine the weight and type of their caseload (Harrison 1988). Even when well-meaning, physicians have been more concerned with the *process* of trying to help patients rather than the outcome; to 'travel hopefully rather than to arrive' as one professor of cardiology put it (Hampton 1983). Yet, even disregarding the conceptual problems of such a notion, complete freedom is hardly imaginable in practice; arguing that physicians should adhere to a code of conduct, Fox (1951, quoted in Hoffenberg 1992: 3–4) imagined its absence:

> A man or boy [*sic*] wishes to be a doctor. Having learnt as much or as little as he pleases, he can see whatever patients consult him, when it suits him; he can give whatever advice he pleases, however unorthodox, and provide whatever treatment he pleases, however expensive or lethal; he can behave towards his patients however he pleases and extract from them whatever they will pay.

Discussion of clinical freedom cannot simply therefore proceed at the level of rhetoric but must specify the domains of professional behaviour and the constraints that operate in each of these. For the purposes of this chapter, clinical autonomy is a micro-level phenomenon, distinguishable in principle from the social and economic freedoms often enjoyed by physicians (Schulz and Harrison 1986). In the UK, these latter freedoms are to some extent the manifestation of macro level sources of medical influence, exerted through close corporatist relationships between the British Medical Association (BMA) and the Department of Health (Doehler 1989; Harrison *et al.* 1990: Ch. 4: see also Groenwegan and Calnan 1995). The micro-level practices are supported by the macro-level too; for instance, it is national negotiating mechanisms that gave UK hospital specialists ('consultants') lifetime tenure and formal rights to make public comment, even in criticism of their employer. These rights exemplify successful claims to be unmanaged. For half a century the NHS manifested both a policy and the practice of clinical autonomy. Such manifestations can be summarized under three headings.

First, *commitment to clinical autonomy* has figured fairly prominently in the official pronouncements of governments (of both Conservative and Labour persuasion) since the period, during the Second World War, when post-war health service organization was under consideration. The wartime coalition government's 1944 White Paper stated that 'whatever the organization, the doctors taking part must remain free to direct their clinical knowledge and personal skill for the benefit of their patients in the way which they feel to be best' (Ministry of Health 1944: 26). These sentiments were subsequently echoed on several occasions by Aneurin Bevan, the Minister of Health who presided over the inception of the NHS (Watkin 1975; Allsop 1984). The same view was manifest by both main political parties in the preparations for the first reorganization of the NHS in 1974; Labour policy was that 'the Service should provide full clinical freedom to the doctors working in it' (DHSS 1970: 29), while the Conservative line specified that 'professional workers will retain their clinical freedom . . . to do as they think best for their patients' (DHSS 1972a: vii), noting in a subsequent document that 'management plays only a subsidiary part . . . [it] can help or hinder the people who play the primary part' (DHSS 1972b: 9). As recently as 1979 it was stated (by the then newly elected Conservative government) that 'It is doctors, dentists and nurses and their colleagues in the other health professions who provide the care and cure of patients and promote the health of the people. It is the purpose of management to support them in giving that service' (DHSS and Welsh Office 1979: 1–2).

Second, many aspects of the NHS's *formal organization* have long been constructed in a way which is consonant with clinical autonomy for doctors. Thus GPs have the status of self-employed business persons under a rather vaguely worded contract for services to the NHS; 'A doctor shall render to his [sic] patients all necessary and appropriate personal medical services of the kind usually provided by general medical practitioners' (Ellis and Chisholm 1993: 12). Until recently (see below) GPs were entitled to refer patients to any specialist in any hospital anywhere in the UK, and (subject to administrative intervention in only the most extreme cases) to prescribe from the pharmacopoeia in whatever quantities they chose. Moreover, doctors (especially hospital specialists) dominated the management of the NHS, not in the sense of being formally responsible for it, but in the sense of having an entrenched and effective veto. Thus the then statutory bodies within the NHS (such as Regional Hospital Boards and Hospital Management Committees) had large numbers of doctors in membership (Ham 1981) until 1974, after which (until 1984) the NHS was managed by multidisciplinary consensus decision-making teams of which (at the key operational level) doctors, each with the power of veto, constituted half the membership (for a review, see Harrison 1982). The strong corporatist relationship between government health departments and the BMA has contributed to workforce planning practices very much in the profession's interests (Harrison 1981; Harrison *et al.* 1990: Ch. 4); consultant contracts of employment has also been carefully insulated from managerial discretion by being held at the regional, rather than operational, level of organization, and include a number of unilaterally exercisable rights, including that of private practice, and that of appeal to the Secretary of State against dismissal.

Third, the *practice of management* in the NHS over the period until the late 1980s has been likened to the practice of diplomacy. Rather than conforming to the 'textbook' managerial stereotype of an authoritative individual, rationally pursuing organizational objectives by means of proactively generated change, the NHS manager possessed little influence relative to doctors, was very much focused on responding to the demands of internal organizational actors, and procured only incremental change. Summarizing the evidence from some 25 empirical studies conducted up to 1983, the present author concluded that:

> Managers neither were, nor were supposed to be, influential with respect to doctors. The quality of management (like the quality of the

service itself) was judged by its inputs. Managers in general worked to solve problems and to maintain their organizations rather than to secure major change.

(Harrison 1988: 51)

Although managerial reforms (including the replacement of consensus teams with general managers/chief executives) begun after the Griffiths Report (NHS Management Inquiry 1983; for a summary, see Harrison 1988: Ch. 4) clearly offered something of a challenge to clinical autonomy, a review of empirical research carried out between 1984 and 1990 concluded that, despite defeats over the *form* of the Griffiths innovations, the medical profession had experienced little, if any, resulting loss of autonomy. These findings correspond to the observation that, *so far as doctors were concerned*, the 'diplomat' role for managers had not changed much (Harrison *et al.* 1992: Ch. 4). One change which occurred for managers, however, was that they became much more *externally focused*; they were increasingly compelled to respond to governmental agendas and were consequently less able to respond to internal professional agendas (Flynn 1988; Williamson 1990).

The remainder of this chapter is divided into three main sections. The first outlines, in the context of recent academic arguments about changes in the professional power of medicine, some of the present challenges to clinical freedom which arise from the post-1991 introduction of the quasi-market and associated organizational changes within the NHS. The second section outlines some outcomes of these challenges in terms of shifts of power and autonomy within the UK medical profession. The final section suggests the elements of an explanation as to why clinical freedom has been so pervasive a phenomenon for medical practice in the NHS, and assesses the implications of this explanation for the future of professional autonomy in UK health policy.

The challenge of health service reforms

Medicine is not alone among professions in facing challenges apparently stemming from managerial activity but which arise more fundamentally from the gradual withdrawal of the state as guarantor of professional status (Johnson 1993; for a comparison of physicians and lawyers, see Brazier *et al.* 1992). In general, the empirical literature points to tightening administrative and cultural control of a range of professional occupations in a range of countries (Reed and Anthony 1992; Moran and Wood 1993; Bloor and Dawson 1994). Interpretations of the significance of these challenges are, however, diverse. At one extreme is the proletarianization thesis (McKinlay and Arches 1985), which focuses on the increasing tendencies for medicine to be regulated by the state and for doctors to be employed by corporate organizations rather than remaining in independent practice. Such an analysis can be criticized both because it conflates proletarianization and corporatization (Navarro 1988) and because it is United States-centric in assuming that state regulation and self-regulation are distinct, and that physician self-employment has been the norm and brings greater autonomy than salaried practice; the NHS provides a counter-example of both (Schulz and Harrison 1986; Armstrong 1990). At the other extreme are analyses which acknowledge the challenges but interpret them as relatively marginal in their impact on the profession as a whole, consisting rather of shifts of power *within* medicine – that is, developments such as the medically-qualified manager and the use of protocols to control clinical activity (Freidson 1985; Mechanic 1991). In their turn, such arguments have been criticized both for failing to take account of the likelihood that a physician-manager will behave like a manager rather than remaining a 'true' professional, and for other alleged equivocations over the nature of a professional occupation (Coburn 1992).

Though not in quite such polarized form as set out above, there are similar ongoing disputes specifically about challenges to medicine in the NHS, often cast in the language of Alford's (1975) analysis: whether or not it remains the 'dominant interest' or whether it has been superseded as such by the 'challenging interest' of the 'corporate rationalizers', namely management. It is clear that the introduction to the NHS, from 1991, of the purchaser–provider split and associated changes proposed in the White Paper *Working for Patients* (Department of Health *et al.* 1989) and subsequent working papers, presents a series of further challenges, going beyond those arising from the Griffiths Report, to the clinical freedom of NHS doctors, especially hospital consultants. (For a detailed account of the organizational changes, see Levitt and Wall 1992; Ham 1994.) These challenges may be loosely divided into those which emanate from the purchasing function of the new NHS (namely, health authorities, purchasing commissions and consortia, and fundholding GPs) and from the response of providers (namely, NHS Trusts) to the existence of purchasers.

Challenges from purchasing

Health authorities (HAs) are ostensibly responsible for identifying and prioritizing the health care needs of a geographically defined population before entering into contracts with NHS Trusts for the provision of services to meet such needs. It is clear that the priorities identified may conflict with the desires of clinical doctors to provide particular services for particular patients, especially as the development of expensive new technologies places pressure on budgets. There is, therefore, the possibility of a shift towards *explicit rationing*, away from the earlier practice of implicit rationing through clinical decisions and hospital waiting lists (Harrison and Hunter 1994). In practice, and despite some widely-publicized examples (Freemantle and Harrison 1993; Price 1996), HAs have for the most part avoided such explicit decisions in favour of simply indicating low priorities and restricted availability of particular interventions, thus leaving it to clinicians to select the patients who would, and would not, receive them (Harrison and Wistow 1992). However, since HAs are financially liable for referrals made by non-fundholding GPs within the district, the freedom of such GPs to refer is now constrained to providers with whom the HA is in contract, unless an ad hoc 'extra-contractual referral' is sanctioned by the HA (Johnston 1994).

Purchasing authorities are not only concerned with what services are provided, but may also seek to exert control over how they are provided. There are reported cases of actual or threatened removal of contracts as a response to HA or GP fundholder dissatisfaction with standards (Glennerster *et al.* 1994). GP fundholders have also been able to use their leverage as purchasers to enforce changes in consultants' work arrangements, such as the introduction of specialist outreach clinics on GPs' practice premises (Dixon and Glennerster 1995; Petchey 1995). In addition, there is now government pressure (NHS Executive 1996a) on purchasers to seek the implementation of medical practice based on research into clinical efficacy: so-called 'evidence-based medicine'. This is likely to lead to increased reliance on clinical guidelines and protocols as a means of seeking more systematized medical practice (Harrison 1994a).

Challenges from provider managers

In a quasi-market situation, provider managers need a means of controlling their organization's output so as to allow the terms of the contracts into which they have entered to be met. This has led to a range of internal line-managerial arrangements which have built upon the general management changes introduced by the Griffiths Report. Thus all Trusts have a medical director, and many have internal organizations built around 'clinical directorates' headed by consultants (often working closely with a senior manager), as well as 'resource management', that is, budgets for clinicians (Packwood *et al.* 1991, 1992). In essence, these are attempts to use doctors to manage other doctors and to persuade doctors to think in more managerial terms by placing budgetary constraints on them and by encouraging them to 'rub shoulders' with managers (Harrison and Pollitt 1994). Coupled with managerial access to aggregate medical audit data, these changes make it easier for managers to challenge doctors over their use of resources and the services to which they give priority.

The potential significance of these changes for doctors are to some extent underpinned by the fact that Trust managers have greater control than previously over medical appointments and terms and conditions of employment; they not only now hold contracts of employment locally but may vary some of the terms, for instance by offering fixed-term appointments or by restricting private practice to the Trust's own facilities. In addition, hospital consultants are required to have 'job plans' which specify how the larger part of their working week is to be spent, and managers have been given a role in recommending consultants for the receipt of distinction awards (for a summary, see Moore 1995).

Conflict, compromise or collaboration?

It is too early to say whether the developments described above have resulted in an empirical decline in medical autonomy. Although the NHS's official historian, Charles Webster, has been quoted as saying that management is now the most powerful occupation: 'for consultants, the days of power and prestige are over' (Moore 1995: 27), authors such as Flynn (1992) and Harrison and Pollitt (1994) have concluded from their reviews of the evidence that there has certainly been a shift in that direction, but have stopped short of concluding that management is now the dominant interest. It is also rather difficult to make unequivocal distinctions between conflict, compromise and collaboration in these relationships because so many of the challenges outlined above can be read as attempts at *incorporation*, that is, as aimed at the inculcation in professionals of managerial values and cognitive structures (Harrison and Pollitt 1994: Ch. 4).

In any case, however, there are some obvious factors which must limit any managerial ascendancy. One is the impending shortage of UK-trained doctors for many specialties. Another is the continuing centrality of doctors in the hospital workflow, which gives them a good deal of collective influence (Hinings *et al.* 1971) provided that they display a degree of solidarity; in recent disputes in Brighton, Burnley and Staffordshire, it is managers who have been the casualties (Moore 1995). It is also far from self-evident that the policies described above were specifically intended to diminish clinical autonomy. Although the policies of an anti-statist and anti-trade union (of which the professions were held simply to be a particularly well-entrenched example) government developed at the time of a massive budget deficit (Harrison 1994b; Harrison and Pollitt 1994: Ch. 2), they are also examples of 'policymaking on the hoof' (Paton 1992; Harrison 1994b) in that they developed incrementally and often accidentally rather than explicitly. What, though, do they mean for clinical autonomy?

Redistributions of autonomy and dominance

It is clear from the above account that a good deal (though by no means all) of what is actually occurring is a redistribution of autonomy *within* the medical profession, both in ways observed by Friedson in the

United States (Freidson 1985) and others, rather than simply a loss of autonomy to some outside group such as management. At present, three developments seem particularly likely to have pervasive effects: total general practice fundholding, the growth in numbers and responsibilities of managerial doctors, and the implementation of evidence-based medicine.

Total general practice fundholding

In so-called 'total fundholding' (or total purchasing from primary care: TPPC), general practices (usually though not invariably organized in consortia) take over from the HA the financial liability for purchasing virtually all or most forms of secondary and tertiary care for patients registered with the relevant practices. This is a much greater liability, and corresponding autonomy, than that borne by the ordinary GP fundholder. Four locally developed pilot schemes were introduced in 1994–5, and almost 100 further nationally developed schemes – the largest of which will encompass almost 100,000 patients – will be introduced over the period 1995–7 (*Fundholding* 21 February 1996: 5).

Clearly, it is too early to know exactly how these developments will operate, but two dimensions of change seem predictable. First, TPPC further enhances the power of GPs to secure changes in the services provided by hospital consultants. The results might be even more outreach clinics, more direct GP access to diagnostic and therapeutic services (such as echocardiography or physiotherapy) currently controlled by consultants, and perhaps eventually the referral of patients for consultant opinion *only*, rather than with the currently implied request to treat if considered necessary. Government priority for a 'primary care-led' NHS (NHS Executive 1996a), changes in medical technology (which, for instance, allow various pathology tests to be undertaken in general practice by the use of kits) and the de facto development of informal clinical specialisms within general practice are factors which suggest that consultants will find it difficult to recover lost ground. Second, the development of TPPC seems to offer the possibility of a substitution of individual clinical judgement about patient need for the more population-based decisions made by HAs. Although this should not of itself be equated with implicit rationing, it certainly offers the possibility of a shift back in that direction, though with decisions now in the hands of GPs that would have previously been in the hands of consultants.

In summary, one dimension of the redistribution of autonomy within the medical profession is from consultants to GPs: as noted above, a transfer already begun with ordinary fundholding. This shift has been summed up in a joke current in the NHS, that GPs now expect to receive Christmas cards from consultants rather than vice versa; it is likely to continue given the commitment of recent White Papers (see for instance

Department of Health *et al.* 1996) to a primary care-led NHS. Although it is possible to overstate the extent to which UK GPs operate as independent professionals (though self-employed, their remuneration and conditions of work are heavily regulated by government), there is a sense in which the shift of power to them represents something of a move *away* from the international trend of increasing corporatization of medicine.

Managerial doctors

Reference has already been made to the development of 'managerial doctors' within hospitals: medical directors and clinical directors. In general terms this development is not new; medical superintendents were commonplace in chest hospitals until the 1950s and psychiatric hospitals until the 1970s, and the Griffiths managerial reforms of the mid-1980s provided for general manager/chief executive posts to be open to applicants of any discipline. What is new is rather that each Trust is *required* to have a medical director, and that in larger Trusts the post is full-time, in some cases occupied by physicians who have no intention of returning to clinical practice. In the specific context of the UK, where collegiate values and the perception that all consultants were peers has long provided a marked contrast to the more hierarchical arrangements within US medicine, this represents a significant cultural change; in the past 'administrative' doctors were generally regarded as failed clinicians, whereas management is now gradually becoming perceived as a legitimate later career option. It seems likely that the same kind of developments will occur within total fundholding; among a consortium of 30 or 40 GP principals, a de facto managerial hierarchy seems bound to emerge.

Hence a second dimension of the redistribution of autonomy is between 'ordinary' clinicians and medical managers, though the latter may well continue to undertake some clinical work. Such a change is partially underpinned by changes in both undergraduate and postgraduate medical education, where management is increasingly taught and examined as a compulsory subject.

Evidence-based medicine

Reference has already been made to the government policy of evidence-based medicine, which is underpinned by a large NHS research and development programme (Baker and Kirk 1996). Central assumptions of this policy are that the evidence derived from research can, and should, be introduced into routine clinical practice, and that normative clinical guidelines provide an important means of achieving this (NHS Executive 1996b). This implies a redistribution of autonomy between those who construct these definitions of the orthodox and those rank-and-file clinicians (in both hospital and general practice) who are supposed to follow them, though it can be argued that implementation is by no means the straightforward issue of distillation and communication that the notion of guidelines implies (Harrison 1994a). Loosely speaking, this redistribution of autonomy is from ordinary clinicians to medical academics. It represents more, however, than just a transfer between different actors; it also implies a shift of prevailing epistemology, away from a deterministic one based in laboratory research towards a probabilistic one based on analytical statistics – from realism to empiricism, as Tanenbaum (1994) puts it (see also Harrison 1996).

The above changes have already begun to take place. More speculatively, some other shifts within medicine are possible. For instance, it is possible to envisage the growth of 'career' (i.e. non-training) grades of doctor other than consultant or GP principal, in other words the development of a hierarchical division of labour within medicine. This exists currently in minor forms such as the 'staff doctor', but the needs of Trust management to provide a predictable service which meets contracts with purchasers might (if allowed by government) allow routine medical work to be delegated to staff with less autonomy than currently enjoyed by consultants. Given the absence of a surplus of UK-trained doctors, overseas graduates might be early candidates for such a role, in much the same way as they were consigned to earlier sub-consultant grades (Jones 1981). Even more speculatively, it is possible to predict a redistribution of autonomy within medical specialties. Apparently perversely, this redistribution would be *towards* those specialties, such as surgery, whose output is relatively easily measured because it consists of discrete interventions. In a quasi-market situation, a great deal of legitimacy is derived from one's activities being measurable; measurability, though it allows one's performance to be observed, also allows one to defend oneself. The existing hierarchy of medical specialties tends already to place at the top specialties such as surgery, so that this final dimension of redistribution would only affect currently low-status specialties whose work is measurable (genito-urinary medicine, for instance) and vice versa (neurology, for instance).

Explaining clinical freedom

The developments described above represent both change and continuity: change within the medical profession but continuity in terms of the profession's relationship with other actors. As a collection of workers possessing medical qualifications, UK doctors have maintained their professional autonomy at a time when the cost pressures associated with publicly financed health services might have been expected to leave the managers (Alford's 'corporate rationalizers') in the ascendant. In explaining this, it does not seem helpful to engage in essentialist disputes about the 'true' nature of professionalism, about (for instance) whether medical managers are really just ordinary managers in disguise, or whether the writers of clinical guidelines are just a new form of bureaucrat. It is not simply that doctors have fought a successful rearguard action, though of course the events in Brighton, Burnley and Staffordshire referred to above are examples of such action. Rather, clinical freedom in a general sense has continued to be supported by public policy, and one might ask why this has been so.

Discussions of clinical autonomy are often polarized: either, to put it crudely, it is seen as the means by which a doctor does his or her best for the patient; or else it is seen as a strategy by which doctors contrive an easy life for themselves. In fact, these two positions are not incompatible, and there is also a third, equally compatible, position. In this final main section, the politics of clinical freedom are analysed in order to suggest why it has proved so durable in face of the challenges previously described. The account is structured around three perspectives, each of which is drawn from a different sociological perspective on the concept of professionalism (Harrison and Pollitt 1994: Ch. 1), and each of which functions in a particular way for a particular social actor: for patients, doctors and the state respectively.

Clinical freedom as medical ethics

In any health system which relies upon third-party payment, a tension arises which is not present with out-of-pocket payment: a clash of interest between patient and third-party payer. The doctrine of clinical autonomy is the means of resolving this tension; it provides that, within broader or narrower limits, and subject to patient consent, the physician will be free to act in the patient's interests rather than, say, in accordance with some utilitarian calculus (Hoffenberg 1987: 17). Thus although this particular view of clinical autonomy is espoused and articulated by the medical profession, often couched as an ethical statement, it is *patients* who would expect to benefit. The British Medical Association advises its members thus:

> resources are finite and this may restrict the freedom of the doctor to advise his [*sic*] patient . . . [and thus] infringes the ordinary relationship between patient and doctor . . . The doctor has a general duty to advise on equitable allocation and efficient utilisation [but this] is subordinate to his professional duty to the individual who seeks his clinical advice.
>
> (British Medical Association 1980: 35)

It is thus an important political symbol for a National Health Service which is claimed by statute to be comprehensive; as *The Patient's Charter* puts it,

The Government believes that there must be no change to the fundamental principles on which [the NHS] was founded and on which it has continued ever since, namely that services should be available to *every citizen* on the basis of clinical need, regardless of ability to pay.

(Department of Health 1991: 4, emphasis in original)

In addition to its ostensible guarantee of an ethical approach which gives priority to the individual patient, this view of clinical freedom also trades upon the assumption that because a doctor's expertise is esoteric (Millerson 1964) only free decision making by him or her can ensure that what is advised is what is best for the patient.

Clinical freedom as professional dominance

A consequence of autonomy is that it brings both intellectual and material benefits to physicians. Depending upon the particular health system (for an international comparison, see Schulz and Harrison 1986), clinical autonomy may permit the choice of practice type and location, of clinical interest and treatment modes, of workload and of the logistics of working life. Clinical freedom claims superiority for medicine over the other health professions (Tolliday 1978) and, as was seen above, helps to determine the character of NHS management, perhaps suggesting that Coburn's (1992) distinction between autonomy and dominance is not so clear-cut. It is both an outcome of occupational advancement and a means of sustaining that advancement over time. Expressed in more general terms, professional dominance is achieved by the conversion of the political into the neutral and technical (Johnson 1993: 150) in order to confer the legitimacy of expertise on doctors' decisions and activities.

Evidence from the UK suggests that doctors do not have fixed views about the appropriate boundaries of clinical freedom (Harrison *et al.* 1984); rather, it functions as a rhetorical device, to be employed in the face of perceived threats. Indeed, this was exactly how the British Medical Association responded to the Griffiths general management proposals of the mid-1980s (Harrison 1994b): 'If [a manager] took decisions which were harmful to our patients then we would not feel bound to co-operate with him [*sic*] in carrying out that decision' (Mr Anthony Grabham, then Chairman of BMA Council, giving evidence to the House of Commons Social Services Select Committee, 18 January 1984).

It is this view of clinical freedom which underpins criticism by academic social scientists and by managers, even though, as will be seen, it may be in the interests of the latter. But it is primarily *doctors* who benefit from these aspects of autonomy.

Clinical freedom as a rationing device

Despite what has been said above there are at least two important senses in which clinical freedom is not freedom at all. One is that medical judgements are not just spontaneously produced by doctors; in whole or part they depend on socialization internalized during professional training, including the 'medical model'. As Esland (1980: 255) has noted, occupations such as medicine are *normative* in that the thrust of their work is towards helping individuals readjust to the requirements of their society. Thus the physician cannot react to his or her patient's asbestosis by issuing a prescription for factory closure.

Second, resources are finite and the doctor cannot prescribe everything from which his or her patients and potential patients might benefit. In third-party payment systems, therefore, and despite the formal ethics, doctors *ration* health care, even where they perceive that the benefits of doing more for a patient might be slight (Harrison and Hunter 1994). In his classic analysis of 'street-level bureaucracy', Lipsky notes that this process of squeezing the infinite into the finite is true for all welfare professions: doctors, social workers, teachers, police and so on:

> At best, street-level bureaucrats invent benign modes of mass processing that more or less permit them to deal with the public fairly, appropriately and successfully. At worst, they give in to favouritism, stereotyping and routinising – all of which serve private or agency purposes.
>
> (Lipsky 1980: xii)

One result of this is that there are limits to the extent to which such welfare agencies can be controlled in the ordinary managerial sense; quite literally, the professionals make up the 'product' as they go along:

> the decisions of street-level bureaucrats, the routines they establish, and the devices they invent to cope with uncertainties and work pressures, effectively *become* the public policies they carry out.
>
> (Lipsky 1980: xii, emphasis in original; see also
> Harrison and Pollitt 1994: Ch. 6)

It is easy to see how these two factors work for the benefit of *government and the state*. First, they confine the apparent causes of, and remedies for, ill health to politically safe ground; crudely, they do not challenge capitalism. This can be seen as the conversion to the technical of a different set of politics from that entailed in professional dominance. Second, though they defeat direct management control, they make politically invisible the process of rationing health care in a system which in theory provides comprehensible care; it is reduced to individual, fragmented and unrecorded transactions between doctors and patients and/or their relatives. This process has been graphically described by two American students of the NHS:

The British physician often seems to adjust his [*sic*] indications for treatment to bring into balance the demand for care and the resources available to provide it. This kind of rationalisation preserves as much as possible the feeling that all care of value is being provided. Most patients in Britain appear willing to accept their doctor's word if he says that no further treatment of a particular disease is warranted.

(Aaron and Schwartz 1984: 111)

Concluding comments

The above analysis makes clear why clinical freedom has been so persistent and pervasive in the NHS. Simply, there has been something in it for all the main players. It does not matter that these actors value it for different reasons (Lindblom 1979); although the three perspectives outlined above are very different from each other, they are not contradictory in terms of their policy implications. All speak powerfully for the retention of clinical autonomy; it is perceived to have advantages for both patients, doctors and governments and is therefore a powerful source of legitimization for the NHS. Moreover, such appeal is based on a broad view of what constitutes a doctor, namely someone who is unconcerned with the redistributions of dominance and autonomy described above.

Given the importance of clinical freedom in the legitimization of NHS decision making, it is worth considering the potential consequences of its decline. Clinical autonomy is a politically unobtrusive method for the inevitable rationing of health care. The whole functionality of this approach to rationing is, of course, undermined if the process becomes explicit. But this is increasingly what is happening as a result of the purchaser–provider split. Although most explicit rationing to date has been in respect of high profile but (in the context of the total NHS) marginal services such as cosmetic surgery, assisted conception and varicose vein surgery (Harrison and Wistow 1992), the problem is becoming more pervasive. Denied arterial surgery on the grounds that he smoked, a Wakefield man was reported to observe:

I have worked since I was 14 up until recently and paid a hell of a lot in taxes to the government, both in income taxes and on the 40 cigarettes a day I smoked. Surely it is not too much for me to ask to have an operation that might ease my pain in my old age and make me live a little longer.

(*Yorkshire Evening Post* 26 August 1993: 1)

In addition, many hospitals have been either unwilling or unable (which, it is not clear) to spread their contracted caseload evenly throughout the financial year, resulting in much-publicized restrictions on routine cases, and cancellations of patients already booked for admission. At least one hospital has developed an explicit system of scoring clinical priority, which would result in some patients never being treated (Giles 1993).

Such explicit managerial rationing would undermine confidence in the NHS, or indeed the UK welfare state more generally. It is clear from several surveys that the public regards doctors, rather than either politicians or NHS managers, as the legitimate decision makers about the availability of treatments on the NHS (Heginbotham 1993; Bowling 1996). The NHS has been an important source of what analysts such as O'Connor (1973) and Offe (1984) regard as the legitimization of the capitalist state in the UK. If this line of analysis is of any validity, then the decline of clinical autonomy would contribute to a more generalized crisis of government.

Yet it seems that the maintenance of clinical autonomy has its price too. The more-or-less peaceful redistribution of dominance and autonomy within the medical profession may not proceed indefinitely. One possible outcome is the kind of 'internal combustion' suggested by Freidson (1994) in which identity (both self-perceived and publicly perceived) as a professional becomes of much-diminished importance. On the other hand, it is possible that the brute facts of daily, fairly autonomous clinical practice will reassert themselves in the face of a bureaucracy whose resources are threatened by public and political antipathy to such expenditure.

To conclude: this chapter is a beginning rather than an end. Its tentative thesis is that the continued legitimization of the NHS in the context of financial pressures upon the welfare state can be achieved by a modification of the form of professional autonomy: its redistribution among different groups of doctors. In terms of this argument, the key fact is that, as Mechanic (1991: 495) has pointed out, the changes within the profession all fall within a continuing medical paradigm and therefore perpetuate its intellectual dominance even if the autonomy of particular groups is under challenge; thus there is still a growing medicalization of personal and social problems and growing media interest in biomedical advances. Indeed, the source of any challenge to this paradigm is precisely not from health service management, but would be from alternative paradigms such as certain complementary therapies. The analysis conducted here has relied upon a fairly crude conception of clinical autonomy, and does not attempt to explain the precise forms newly taken by clinical freedom. An agenda for further enquiry which starts not from doctors, but from public policy, is implied.

5 | Markets and management: the case of primary schools

Ian Menter and Yolande Muschamp

Introduction

Primary schools are relatively small institutions, typically employing between ten and 30 people in a variety of roles. The education 'reforms' of the Conservative governments from 1988 through to the mid-1990s have had an enormous impact. In this chapter we draw on a research project carried out during this period to examine the changing nature of schoolwork in the primary sector.

The first section explores the education policy context at this time. We then describe our project and outline some of the themes which are pertinent to the concerns of this book. We consider in turn three groups of workers – head teachers, teachers and school secretaries. Our conclusion summarizes some of the major shifts which have taken place in work relations in primary schools.

Policy context

After the Education Reform Act of 1988 it became commonplace in the study of education policy to suggest that there were two major strands to the government's policy. On the one hand were what might be called the educational process elements. These would include the National Curriculum and national assessment arrangements. On the other hand were the structural elements. These elements of policy concerned the governance and finance of schools, including open enrolment, local management (LMS) and 'opting out' (to grant-maintained status). These two strands could be seen to represent each of the two sets of ideologies which were taken to comprise the thinking of the 'New Right'. The process strand thus represented the moral authoritarian tendency, with its emphasis on tradition, nation and the family. The structural strand on the other hand represented the economic libertarianism tendency, with its commitment to the free market and competition.

As Whitty (1989) was quick to point out, however, the idea that there was a deep contradiction between these two elements was not borne out in the enactment of the policies. It has become increasingly clear with the passage of time that the two strands complement each other in an effective way. The process elements contribute to the idea of a common good or product, the quality of which varies according to the diversity among producers. This quality can be judged by various performance indicators. The two key mechanisms for judging performance are the so-called league tables and the inspection of schools. The first of these has of course met considerable opposition (and not only from teachers). Tests have now been implemented in primary schools, and school performance tables comparing schools are being introduced. The new inspection arrangements, which were actually brought in through the 1992 Education Act, will lead to the publication of reports on all schools.

When one reviews education policy development as a whole, over the years 1988–95, although there has been considerable resistance, chaos and confusion at times, nevertheless it is possible to identify a coherent push for a market-based approach to state education. This marketization is in fact a more comprehensive spread of policies than has sometimes been recognized by the economic analyses of the 'quasi-market' school (see Le Grand and Bartlett 1993; Bartlett *et al.* 1994).

Much recent education policy research has focused either implicitly or explicitly on the secondary school sector (see for example Ball 1990; Bowe and Ball 1992; Fitz *et al.* 1993; Ball 1994). This is regrettable for it is apparent that there are a number of significant differences between the primary and secondary schools as sites of sociological study. The most obvious difference is the different scale of the institutions. The typical primary school is approximately a fifth of the size of a typical secondary school, in terms of pupil numbers. The size of the workforce is (approximately) proportionally lower. The gender composition of the workforce, particularly the teachers, is significantly different, with more than 80 per cent women, compared with approximately 50 per cent in the secondary sector. It has also been suggested that there are considerable cultural differences in the management and organization of primary schools.

In this paper we report some findings from a project, one aim of which was to remedy this omission in previous research. After giving a brief description of the project's design, we consider firstly aspects of the management of primary schools, before then considering questions of professional autonomy, particularly as manifested in the experiences of teachers and school secretaries.

The project

The project from which this chapter derives[1] explores the impact of marketization on the management of primary schools in an English county town.

The city was chosen because it was small enough to be studied as a single discrete market. As in most small cities there was a wide range of primary schools reflecting the pattern of housing across the city, from old Victorian buildings at the centre to newly built green site schools in the recently constructed suburbs. In parts of the town, urban renewal and redevelopment were leading to disturbance in residential patterns as established communities were rehoused and dispersed to different parts of the city. In addition to this the local newspaper had obtained and published confidential results of the first Key Stage 1 national assessment results (an assessment of all 7-year-olds in state primary schools) to create their own city league tables. Consequently the teachers of the city schools had some early experience of responses to publication of school performance data and a preview of the likely impact of government policies.

After a survey of the enrolment patterns of the 32 city schools, 12 had been selected for visits and interviews with the head teachers. From an analysis of these interviews, two schools, one junior (with children aged 8–11 years) and the other primary (with pupils aged 4–11 years) were chosen for case study over 15 months.

A major aim of the project was to ascertain the connections between the apparent marketization of primary education and the nature of work within primary schools. Our main focus was not on the impact of the 'reforms' on the educational experience of pupils. Rather, we wished to explore the relationships between head teachers, teachers and other schoolworkers and the ways in which they experienced and understood their work in this new context. Without exception, head teachers of primary schools in England and Wales are drawn from the teaching workforce. The distinction between managers and professionals which may be relevant in other sectors (private or public) has not been applicable in schools in this country.

Prior to the implementation of the 1988 Education Reform Act, influential research on the management of primary schools indicated that most school staffs functioned in a relatively simple manner, acting more or less as a team, under the leadership of the head teacher. Nias *et al.* (1989) described this as 'a culture of collaboration'. Although teachers were differentiated by salary scale (and later, allowances), this rarely led to visible hierarchical structures within a school's teaching staff, with the exception of the position of the head and sometimes of the deputy head. Teachers had considerable autonomy within their own classrooms, in terms of curriculum, assessment and pedagogy. This was consistent with the ethos and educational ideologies which predominated in the primary sector (Nias 1989; Proctor 1990).

The head teacher was seen as the educational leader of the school, but did not necessarily seek to bring about particular pedagogical approaches. The extent to which the curriculum was planned across the whole school varied quite widely. Resources and staffing, admissions and transfers, were coordinated by the local education authority (LEA). The role of governing bodies was largely advisory, although this had started to change following the Education Act of 1986, which had restructured their composition and increased their visibility.

Since the Education Reform Act 1988, primary schools have had to cope not only with enormous curricular and assessment innovation, but also with a raft of new management and governance policies. These have included the devolution of financial control, new powers and responsibilities for governors, open enrolment and the possibility of becoming grant-maintained. Furthermore, the introduction of whole-school planning, appraisal and, in some places, local bargaining and performance-related pay, indicate a shift in the nature of staff management and labour relations in schools. All these changes – these multiple innovations (Wallace 1992) – could be described collectively as bringing about a 'new management' in primary education, replacing the frequently paternalistic, unfocused and implicit practices of the old.

The avowed purpose of introducing competitive practices, in short the marketization of primary and secondary education, is to improve the performance of schools. But as Stephen Ball (1990) has pointed out, these changes bring with them a development in the functioning of schools towards a business culture: 'The model of organisation which the ERA [1988 Education Reform Act] implies is clear: it is that of governors as Board of Directors and headteacher as Chief Executive' (Ball 1990: 67).

One of the largest studies of the impact of the National Curriculum and assessment on English primary schools, the PACE project (Pollard *et al.* 1994), which had a national sample, generated a model of the impact of the requirements which schools faced in the early 1990s. This had arisen in an attempt to explain empirical findings about varying degrees of continuity and change in the experience of head teachers, teachers and pupils within primary schools. One important finding, for instance, was that there has been relative continuity in pupils' classroom experience, while teachers have struggled to accommodate to considerable change and head teachers have faced even more pressures from external forces and new responsibilities. One way of describing this conceptually is as a continuum flowing from turbulence in the external environment to relative stability in pupil experience, with teachers and head teachers acting as 'mediators'.

Head teachers in the PACE sample saw themselves as being maximally exposed to new legal requirements, management responsibilities for curriculum, staff and finance and new accountability procedures. However, although the inspection threat loomed in many of their thoughts, their commitment to pupils and the idea of staff collegiality meant that they actively sought to face external pressures and, in some sense, to protect staff from them. This, of course, reflects something of the ideological commitments to personal relationships referred to above. However, head teachers did still make many new requirements of their teachers and other staff. There is evidence of agency as well as of strategic response to constraint.

Like class teachers, head teachers have had little choice about whether to implement curricular and assessment innovations. But they have additionally been faced by the range of changes in the governance and management of schools outlined above. New skills have been called for and the nature of head teachers' work has changed at least as much as that of class teachers. The changed role of class teachers has required head teachers to become more directive in their management and more reliant on indicators of performance. The implementation of the National Curriculum alone brought many changes, as traditional conceptions of teacher autonomy had to be challenged in order to provide coherence and progression in the curriculum across the school. The role of the primary head teacher has thus had to develop from that of paternal, educational leader and community servant to that of a manager of a coordinated organization and salesperson of an educational commodity.

Head teachers

This part of the chapter is based on our interviews with the head teachers of our sample of 12 primary schools who were asked about their role as managers and about their perceptions of 'the market'. There are three sections, each dealing with an element of marketization.

Market exposure through open enrolment

Our examination of the history of admissions to the 12 schools (and others) in the county town which is the focus of our study indicated that there was very little active choice being made by parents. The number of children on roll was steady or rising in the majority of schools. In the 33 city schools 18 per cent were experiencing rising rolls, 76 per cent were maintaining their annual intake and 6 per cent were experiencing falling rolls.

Of the 12 heads we interviewed only one acknowledged any change as a direct result of open enrolment, a policy which had been implemented for over a year when the interviews took place. (Open enrolment is the policy which states that parents can choose any school they wish so long as there are places available.) In that school, the roll had increased. Only one head teacher saw parents of the school as 'clients', the others felt this was an inappropriate term to describe them. The majority of heads believed that rather than choosing freely between schools, enrolment patterns reflected the old fixed catchment areas with minimal competition between them.

In those schools where enrolments were below the standard numbers, heads believed this was to do with local demographic change or the construction of new schools. (A school's standard number is the designated pupil capacity of a school – that is, it sets the limit for open enrolment.) All the head teachers supported open enrolment in principle but none thought that it could work in practice under the current arrangements. The reasons given for this were lack of spaces at the popular schools. The new schools were attracting parents but they were full and had waiting lists, therefore parents could not place children in their first-choice school. Nine of the heads expressed disappointment that the parents' expectations had been raised and felt that their school should cater primarily for the children in their locality.

All heads felt able to describe the factors they felt affected parents in their selection of a school. The majority, nine out of 12, felt that parents wanted their children to go to a school near to their home. They believed that parents found out about the reputation of schools from their neighbours and friends and that this also influenced their decision. The reputation could relate to a number of factors, including standards of academic performance, social class composition of the pupils or pupil behaviour within the school. The third factor mentioned was the physical environment. More than half the heads felt that parents were attracted to new schools because they presented a bright, cheerful and aesthetically pleasing environment. The existing roll of parents supported the heads' view that parents were choosing the school nearest to their home with the exception of the newly built schools. Each school had a few exceptional families who for varying reasons, brought their children to the school from further away.

There was a small number of additional features of each school which the head teachers felt might influence parents, though only marginally. These included: family centres for preschool children, religious ethos, infant transfer and class size. Heads of four schools thought they were in some competition with other nearby schools. Only one saw this as outright competition. The others, most of whom had no shortage of applications from parents, were concerned at the potential damage of competition.

To summarize so far, there was little or no evidence that schools were actually being damaged by competitive market forces.

Nevertheless it emerged that a considerable amount of marketing activity was going on. Nine of the 12 said that they had carried out activities which were designed to attract parents to the school. Of the three that did not, two felt that they had no need to do so and the third felt strongly that resources should not be wasted in this way.

There was great variety in the activities that heads described. Most of them aimed to build a good reputation for the school in the community.

Those that were mentioned most often were: keeping in touch with the local press for coverage of school events; welcoming parents into the school for parents' evenings, to help in classrooms, to a special parents' room or to shows and assemblies; a good quality school prospectus and regular letters home; and maintaining a pleasant, aesthetically pleasing environment.

So heads were willing to act to some degree as if a truly competitive market existed. They seem to have done this because they were anxious about competition or because they were legally obliged to (in the case of the preparation of a school prospectus). They were aware that the likely benefits in terms of attracting more children and hence protecting or improving the school's budget were small. Overall, then, there was evidence of growing anxiety about the impact of competition. The effect of this appeared to have brought about internal changes as well as increased concern with the external image of the school in the community.

One head teacher in fact acknowledged explicitly that his school was now a 'business', and this acknowledgement was presented in a jocular manner when asked to confirm that he now described himself as the 'managing director':

> Well, a slightly silly cliché, but in a sense, from a somewhat realistic point of view really, and I think some heads have a problem because they cannot get used to the fact that their job has changed. I mean you are no longer, for the want of a better term, the sort of school's senior teacher.
>
> (Head teacher, School J)

This same head had recently given up any curriculum subject leadership responsibility.

The heads all indicated the increased significance of financial planning and management, and some indicated that they received a lot of support in this area from secretarial staff. The 'managing director' of School J, when asked about the clerical staffing in his school, replied that the school has

> One office manager, which is an interesting statement, who is on the highest grade but doesn't quite work full-time. And then we have another assistant secretary who works ten hours a week. The office manager really being our nearest equivalent to a bursar.

It may be noted that both heads who said that their (female) secretary knew more about day-to-day financial affairs than they did were men. (Compare this account with the views of the secretaries later in the chapter.)

The major concern with respect to budgets was staffing levels. Age profiles had become significant; in the three cases where a school was in the process of significant expansion, new staff tended to be newly qualified rather than experienced.

Management structures

The internal management structures in the schools had all been developed in response to the new demands being made of them. However, there was considerable variation in responses and this seemed to be related to the size of school. One or two schools had senior management teams, previously a feature only of secondary schools, but most had some form of sub-grouping, either on an age phase basis or on a curriculum basis, again an unusual arrangement in the days before 1988. For instance:

> We have lower school, heads of department, middle school and upper school. I have a deputy head who has overall curriculum responsibility for the school and we also have a staff development officer for the school . . . And all of those people, whether it be of an administrative nature or of a curriculum nature, also have devolved financial responsibility. So we finance areas of the curriculum, we finance the day-to-day consumable aspects of the curriculum as well.
>
> (Head teacher, School H)

All of the heads referred to a range of meetings which were held in their schools. Several differentiated between meetings dealing with immediate issues and those dealing with longer-term curricular or development planning.

> We have two staff meetings a week. One is to cover the general day-to-day running of the school, the diary, the planning, the events . . . Then on Mondays we have what you could call a curriculum meeting when we review policies or initiate a policy. We will look at the school development plan, we have also had time given to looking at computer programs and personal development, we have people in, say, to talk to staff on stress management, on their own self-esteem. It is a time when I make sure it is a social time as well, I provide sort of tea and cakes and we have a few moments when I also ask them to give me some idea of what has gone well for them in their last week. Infant teachers are very good at running themselves down, maybe that's because it's largely female, that they also need a time to consciously tell people of their successes and things that have gone well.
>
> (Head teacher, School D)

This extract is a cogent exposition of the old and the new – the need to deal with such recent innovations as development plans at the same time as fostering a harmonious if paternalistic culture. The use of phrases such as 'personal development' and 'stress management' exemplifies the accommodation between the old and the new.

There was commonly an acknowledgement of the way in which meetings had changed.

[We have a meeting] every Thursday, with a regular very meat-filled meeting. Nothing is allowed to fester, things come out. When you think about it – have you ever taught? – in [town where head worked previously] we had a staff meeting once a term, incredible, they got away with murder. And Tuesday afternoon the head would swan off to the Rotary and we wouldn't see him again until the next day. He was a nice bloke and he was a fairly good head, you know, but I would have been bored out of my head, I think.

(Head teacher, School B)

All of the heads had drawn up development plans. Although advice from the LEA was that plans should cover three years, a number of heads indicated that only an annual cycle was realistic. For example:

I try to do three-year plans but I don't find them successful at all because so much happens in the space of 12 months that you have got to revise it all again, so for the present year, it is just a 12-month plan and I shall construct another one, August, September, for the next 12 months.

(Head teacher, School G)

With respect to development plans, heads also had different approaches to authorship, involvement and consultation, from those who saw it simplest to do it themselves and persuade the staff and governors that it was right, to those who sought a more interactive, developmental approach.

Elsewhere we have explored the connections between some of the features of management in the new primary school context and the set of practices described as Human Resource Management (Menter *et al.* 1997).

The role of governors

One of the consistent threads in government policy since the early 1980s has been to increase the significance of schools' governing bodies. This has been promulgated in the name of local accountability to the parents and the community a school serves. The formal responsibilities of governing bodies are now considerable and include the curriculum, the employment of staff, the awarding of contracts (for example for catering) and the management of the school's budget. Of course the members of the governing body undertake these responsibilities on an entirely voluntary basis.

We asked head teachers for their views about the roles of their governing bodies. Their responses varied from one extreme to the other:

Interviewer: Are they [the governors] very involved with the school?

Head teacher: Yes, it varies, some are extremely involved, others not
very involved at all, but generally speaking it's a very
supportive governing body.

On the other hand:

[under breath] Prats! The chairman is good, he is the councillor for
the area – very supportive but doesn't interfere. The two community
governors, I really have to get behind, because they always leave it to
me. They all work; they've got jobs. You can't expect too much. The
government has been too optimistic – too much responsibility in the
hands of amateurs.

(Head teacher, School I)

This was one of four heads in the sample who were anticipating imminent retirement.

Most of the schools' governing bodies had up to four sub-committees,
but one head appeared to be moving in the opposite direction:

I have cut down on blooming committees, I will tell you that. I can't
stand waffle and time wasting and there was a lot of that when I
arrived . . . You see the head's job now, as I see it, there is one way of
keeping yourself sane and keeping it all on a rational, reasonable
level. If you can work with your chair of governors you can solve a
lot of problems . . . I know where the school is going. If I make a cock-
up, OK, I carry the can.

(Head teacher, School B)

The phrase 'carrying the can' is one which came up in several interviews (see Menter *et al.* 1995). There is little doubt in heads' minds
that their responsibilities are greater than ever. The heads are very aware
of the potential power of governors and often act to minimize the exer-
tion of that power. Grace has summarized the new scenario for heads
thus:

The power relations of school leadership are shifting away from the
leading professional and towards other groups . . . On the other
hand, the weakening and predicted ultimate disappearance of control from the local state, from the local education authority, appears
to give headteachers a new executive freedom – a new form of enterprise and management empowerment.

(Grace 1995: 23)

The role of head teachers has thus been changing rapidly since the
wave of legislation which commenced in the late 1980s. The impact has
been seen in the way in which they talk about their work and in the practices which they describe. Much of this change is associated with the
sense of an external market which is displayed by the heads, though of
course it would be simplistic to imply that these parallel developments in

management and market ideology are *necessarily* entirely interdependent. We now turn to address the perceptions and experiences of other staff who work in primary schools as responses to marketization have been developed; in particular we examine changes in the autonomy of two groups of education workers, teachers and school secretaries.

Teachers

One of the key debates in the sociology of education work in recent years has been around the notion of proletarianization. The idea that teachers in particular have been under relentless pressure to become 'de-skilled' and 'deprofessionalized' has been explored in the USA notably by Apple (1988) and in the UK by Ozga and Lawn (1981) and Lawn and Ozga (1988). (A recent critique of these concepts is provided by Campbell and Neill 1994a.)

Our analysis of teachers' experience in this study indicates that there has undoubtedly been an enormous intensification of teachers' work; but their own accounts, because of their ambiguity, cannot lead to a simple interpretation of proletarianization. Rather, there is a mixture of de-skilling and of re-skilling. Perhaps the most obvious example of re-skilling comes in the form of assessment procedures, where there has been a great increase in the range of techniques which teachers are expected to utilize.

Our analysis reveals a deep alienation in the work of many teachers. Teachers remain committed to the importance of interpersonal relationships, and have experienced many of the recent changes as an attack on the primacy of their relationship with the children in their class.

The teaching staff in both case study schools perceived an increase of control from within the school and, with it, a loss of support from the LEA. They also felt that they now faced increased workloads and responsibilities often with no additional remuneration, and this caused some anger and demoralization. Further, the teachers believed that their career prospects were reducing; they were therefore moving in this respect towards the position of the secretaries who did not anticipate any promotion or upgrading of their jobs. Additionally however, the teachers, far more than the secretaries, were increasingly required to work towards indicators which inevitably reduced their autonomy.

Teacher concern over the loss of support from the LEA was exacerbated by the proposal in one school to opt for grant-maintained status, a move which could happen even though the staff had not given it their support. In both schools this change in the importance of the LEA was also accompanied by a further reduction in the autonomy of class teachers in the areas of curriculum planning and delivery. The introduction of the National Curriculum had required the teachers to work more collaboratively in groups to coordinate their schemes of work. Although the increased collaboration was welcomed there was regret by the experienced teachers at the inevitable loss of independence. They were also experiencing increased pressure as they were now accountable to their peer group, to subject coordinators and to the head teacher.

The increased workload experienced by the class teachers was also a direct result of the introduction of the National Curriculum and the national assessment arrangements. They were now required to take responsibility for at least one area of the curriculum at a whole-school level. Remuneration for this responsibility came from salary increments ('points') which were allocated to them by the head teachers and school governors. There had been changes, though, in the management structures of the school which also contributed to the increased workload. Among these was the creation of senior management teams. In one school the post of deputy head had not been filled when the deputy moved on to a headship – it had been replaced by the appointment of two members of staff to a senior management team.

Although the financial targets and the standard enrolment numbers were constraints affecting the work of the secretaries, the teachers were affected by many more. They were increasingly finding their work defined and determined by particular directives such as National Curriculum attainment targets, national assessment requirements, league tables, school development plans, Ofsted inspection criteria and staff appraisal. In some respects these procedures were serving as performance indicators. Although the teachers tried to support these initiatives because of the greater accountability and standardization they provided, they felt overburdened by the increased administration, their reduced teaching time and a fear that standards would fall because of the time they felt was wasted, and because of the superficial way they were forced to deliver topics because they had so much to cover.

> But it is generally record keeping and admin I find I get bogged down with. For example, the children do half-termly tests now, but they are marked by the teacher which is something extra to what we used to do, and then they have to be filed away in the appropriate folders. And it is finding time to do silly little jobs like that, you know.
>
> (Teacher interview A47)

The teachers felt that the possibility of moving to other schools was becoming more difficult as they became more expensive; more senior teachers resigned themselves to staying in their current posts. The restrictions now placed on their work by targets and indicators left the teachers feeling that their autonomy was threatened. They regretted the way in which the new policies reduced the time that they could spend with the children in their classes. It was the work they did directly with the children that produced job satisfaction. 'Job satisfaction comes from self-achievement and the response of the children, and parents occasionally. No one else ever tells you you are doing well' (Teacher interview B50).

As our study progressed we found that the teachers presented two very different accounts of their views of the changes, one public, the other confidential. At first teachers attempted in a public role to present the changes in their work as positively as possible; however, as the research progressed, very different accounts of the impact and implementation of the changes were disclosed when the teachers spoke confidentially about their private perceptions of the changes. No forum appeared to exist where the teachers felt able to express these concerns other than in close friendships outside their professional role. The two versions were in such conflict with each other that they appeared to contribute to the stress and demoralization that the teachers experienced. This equivocation is examined further. The dual accounts are compared to the experiences of the teachers in a situation of 'burnout' in Freedman's (1988) discussion of the complexity of conflicts which can lead teachers to 'lash out in angry denial'. Can the dual accounts be explained as the expression of teachers' frustration with the intensification (Apple 1988) of their role?

Although their experiences were similar to those identified nationally (for example in the PACE study, Pollard *et al.* 1994), it was not only an increase in workloads that caused concern but rather that they separated the new responsibilities from what they regarded as 'real teaching'. The changes were not those which they would have chosen and led them to try and defend practices which they felt were under attack.

The main areas identified by the teachers as remaining under their control were the teaching styles they used and their relationship with their children. Their response to change had not been entirely to replace old practices with new but to continue the old and the new, side by side with the inevitable increased workload. In this respect the practices of the case study teachers reflected the findings of the study of teachers by Campbell and Neill (1994b), where despite teachers making a conscientious effort to make reforms work, relatively little curriculum change had occurred. There appeared to be an attempt by the teachers to isolate areas of their work where they felt they remained in control.

The differences between their public and private views of their responsibilities were particularly evident in their explanation of the purposes of the changes that were being introduced. Their perceptions of why changes were introduced showed the conflict which existed between the constant support teachers were required to give to the management view of changes and the private understanding, often cynical, of the reality of the motives behind the management decisions. These tensions – both in their practices and their perceptions of the management motivation – inevitably affected the attitudes of the teachers to their views of teaching as a profession and to their confidence of future prospects. The tensions also reflected the dilemmas identified by Nias (1989: 193) which the teachers in her study faced: 'dilemmas which they face stem from views expressed directly or indirectly . . . Either way, teachers' inevitable inability to fully satisfy their own consciences and their wider audiences leaves them feeling simultaneously under pressure, guilty and inadequate.'

However the teachers in our case study had moved on from this position to expressing anger and frustration at their position (albeit privately), as no professional forum appeared available for such expression.

The government initiatives to introduce a market to primary schools have had a profound effect on the role of the teachers within our two case study institutions. There had been intensification of their work and evidence of increased managerialism through the increased delegation of responsibility; increased control, particularly from the supervisory role of colleagues as curriculum coordinators; and the loss of autonomy through the introduction of an unprecedented amount of institutional objectives and targets in the form of the National Curriculum, national assessment, the publication of school results, reporting to parents, teacher appraisal, school development plans and inspection.

The teachers responded to the changes with dual accounts which both reflected their sincere attempt both to cope with the extra workloads but at the same time to give expression to their frustration and anger at their new position. Their position as women in schools where both heads and deputies were men was seen as significant in their interpretations of their roles. The teachers all remained almost excited with the new innovations which potentially offered so much opportunity for them to contribute professionally to the reshaping of their schools – and yet they were severely restricted in their contribution. As Freedman (1988) identified, teachers were rarely asked to demonstrate their intellectual abilities. This was particularly evident with the senior teachers, who felt that their experience and professional skills were supporting the senior managers but were not being recognized. The increased workload was supervisory in nature and created a position where the traditional autonomy of the teacher in the classroom was under threat. Powerless to control these changes through their practice, the teachers appeared to be attempting to remain in control by providing the real account of what was happening. The teachers' dual accounts seemed to provide the only outlet in a situation where more collaborative working meant that criticism could not be made easily. It was fellow teachers who appeared to be responsible. Their traditional isolation within the classroom had always contributed to teacher autonomy; ironically, now their isolation appeared to contribute frustration to their role. They reassessed their 'defensible space' (Lawn and Ozga 1988) but remained in a conflict where the government initiatives aimed to create a parents' charter for choice and diversity and yet the teachers were denied choice and diversity for themselves.

School secretaries

We noted earlier the comments of head teachers about the increased significance of school secretaries. Because it appeared that they were developing certain management responsibilities, our study looked more closely at them than has originally been intended. In the two case study schools the secretaries now took much greater responsibility for financial management, and it was this aspect of local management of schools which had had a particular effect on them.

Within this LEA there had been an evaluation of the role of secretaries in order to reassess their position on their professional scale and to recognize increased workloads and responsibilities. However, in our two case study schools the head teachers, aware of pressure on their budgets, had been reluctant to recognize the additional work of the two secretaries, which would have allowed them to advance to a higher grade. Under LEA control there had been guidelines which schools followed providing a recommendation for the numbers of hours secretaries were to work, and providing a retainer for school holidays. However, it was now for the head teacher and governors to decide on hours and the holiday retainer had been dropped.

> Many secretaries negotiated with head teachers and have been upgraded to Level 4. With cheque book accounts some have negotiated Level 5. There are discrepancies – some colleagues had been put up to first point of Level 4, but she remained at Level 3 despite becoming Clerk to the Governors.
>
> (Interview B30)

The greatest change in work patterns of the two secretaries was brought about by the management of the school budget as part of LMS. This had previously had been managed by the LEA. 'The main area of responsibility is now finance. It's no longer just answering the phone, dinner, school fund, but all the money, maintaining the budget. Biggest responsibility is working of computer and working out budget levels' (Interview A32, secretary Case study school A).

In one of the case study schools, the increased responsibility for financial management had been accompanied by the introduction of a new computer software package for accounting which had contributed to the pressure for the secretary to become more involved. 'Now it's on the computer it's easier. The head teacher leaves the computer to the secretary. He doesn't know how to use it' (Interview A32, secretary Case study school A).

In both schools the secretaries felt that the introduction of new computer facilities had added considerably to their workload. Both had had to attend training to upgrade their skills. However, neither felt that their new skills were rewarded.

In one of the schools the effect of the new computing facilities had considerably increased the control that the secretary held over the expenditure on resourcing. The class teachers revealed how it was in fact the secretary who decided whether a particular purchase could be made despite having received permission from the head.

Interviewer: So she [secretary] actually decides how the budget is going to be distributed?

Teacher: Well, I think you get the impression that she has quite a big say in it, because quite often you are told by — [head teacher] that you can have all this money for all these things, and the next thing — [secretary] will come in and say there isn't the money.

(Teacher interview A46, Case study school A)

Although financial management dominated the changes that the secretaries were experiencing, there were other effects of marketization. In the second case study school the head teacher had worked closely with the secretary to devise procedures for her role as the school receptionist. Facilities had been provided to accommodate these procedures. There was a newly decorated and carpeted seating area for visitors – mostly parents – and a switchboard arrangement so the head could be informed of arrivals.

The secretaries' wide range of responsibilities reflected the special circumstances of primary schools. The transfer of pupils to secondary schools, the social work, the supervision of classes while a supply teacher was being found or if a teacher was late, the informal role of nurse, were all responsibilities they felt were not taken by secretaries in secondary schools, where there would be a secretary to the head teacher, perhaps a bursar and a computer data entry secretary.

The changes had inevitably had their impact on the morale of the two secretaries. They both described their dismay and frustration at the level at which they were paid. Both felt that their roles more closely matched that of bursar. 'Head teacher and secretary work together on budget, but secretary maintains accounts and gives budget expenditure levels to head teacher and advises when accounts are low and money needs changing from one account to another' (Interview B30, secretary Case study school B).

Also their role in the past had involved close contact and support from the LEA officers. They now feared with the loss of these support services that they were increasingly becoming vulnerable. Initially they had hoped that the increased responsibility to be taken by the head teachers and the school governors would lead to greater reward for the contribution that they made to the school, as both the head and governors knew them and would wish to support such an acknowledgement of their commitment to the school. Unfortunately they realized this was not to be the case and were demoralized. Neither belonged to a union but both had however given serious consideration to joining UNISON. They were taking an interest in UNISON activities but admitted that it was very unlikely that they would join. 'I'm stupid really, I should belong but I don't. I've never really believed in unions, but when I see what now happens over the last few years I feel I should' (Interview A32, secretary Case study school B).

They both worked full-time, working alongside part-time general assistants who also helped with secretarial duties but felt isolated in the school. Both commented that their position as women working for male heads possibly aggravated their position.

Conclusion

There is little doubt, on this analysis, that marketization has produced considerable changes in the management of head teachers and in the work of school staff. In general, this must be seen as a move away from pre-existing notions of collegiality towards an increasingly 'managed' form of organization. Perhaps this was an inevitable consequence of the increased complexity of demands and higher levels of self-reliance now faced by primary schools. Managerialism is certainly one response, with an associated fragmentation of collective values, more overt expressions of conflicts of interest and a gradual development of hierarchy.

We have to be cautious about the generalizability of this analysis for, as described in the introduction, the city on which this study is based was selected because it was at the 'front end' of moves towards marketization. Indeed, the local government had, in some ways, done much to bring about the unusual concentration of opted-out, grant-maintained schools in the area. Competition between schools was thus an established idea in the city, even if, as we have shown, it had far less real effect on pupil numbers. Nevertheless, if developments in these schools can be seen as being ahead of the field, then the consequences of marketization which we have identified may soon be found elsewhere, where the same conditions obtain.

There seems little doubt that marketization reaches far, and English primary schools in the mid-1990s are very different workplaces than they were before the Education Reform Act 1988.

During the introduction of the 1988 and subsequent reforms, considerable tensions were created for all schoolworkers. The values and dispositions which had drawn many of them to their work were being challenged. Many head teachers and teachers were choosing early retirement rather than making the necessary adaptations and adjustments. As the marketized approach to education becomes more established it is likely that a greater proportion of head teachers will feel positive about those aspects of the roles which were found challenging in the early 1990s. Similarly, as more teachers enter schools with a background of initial training in the National Curriculum, assessment, school development planning and so on, the ambivalence detected in our study may decline.

However, the major changes which were taking place during this period must be recorded. What was occurring was a fundamental redefinition of schoolwork. All schoolworkers now have greater elements of management in their work and new forms of control. The educational elements of headship have been eroded and the professional identity of primary teachers – based on the primacy of a class teacher's relationship with the children in her class – has been challenged by new pressures and demands, many of which seem bureaucratic. Finally, school secretaries are emerging as an essential element in the business and financial management of primary schools, although this is rarely formally recognized through their pay and conditions.

Note

1 The 'Markets and Management Project' was funded by the University of the West of England and the National Primary Centre (S) and completed in August 1995. The project team was Ian Menter, Yolande Muschamp, Peter Nicholls, Jenny Ozga and Andrew Pollard. This chapter is partly based on earlier papers prepared by all the members of the team. A full account of the project is provided in Menter *et al.* (1997).

6 | Professionals as managers across the public sector

Gordon Causer and Mark Exworthy

The professional as manager

The thesis that professionals and managers stand in a necessarily antagonistic relationship has, as Exworthy and Halford note (in Chapter 1 above), been a recurrent one in the sociological literature. However, this argument has not been without its critics (see for example Child 1982). As Freidson has emphasized, a key problem with the thesis of managerial–professional conflict is the fact that professional employees are commonly managed by those drawn from within the profession itself, a pattern which has been long established both within the public sector and elsewhere. Consequently, even though managerial controls may entail a loss of autonomy on the part of the individual professional, the fact that managers are either practising professionals or of professional origin may be argued to represent a continuation of the principle of professional control (Freidson 1994: 139). Freidson's argument emphasizes that professions are themselves internally stratified, with a division between the rank-and-file practitioner and the supervisory or managerial professional (the 'administrative elite') (p. 142).

Even this, however, is arguably an oversimplification, implying as it does a simple dichotomy between practising professionals on the one hand and supervisory and managerial professionals on the other. In many settings a hard-and-fast distinction along these lines may be difficult to make for at least three reasons. Firstly, the group of managerial professionals may itself be internally stratified, with variations in the relative closeness of different positions to day-to-day practice. Secondly, a number of areas are characterized by the existence of 'hybrid' roles in which the exercise of formalized managerial responsibilities is carried on alongside continuing engagement in professional practice. Thirdly, the role of the rank-and-file practitioner may itself entail activities of a managerial kind, even where the position occupied is not formally designated as a managerial one. This is most obviously the case where the professional employee has responsibility for supervising the work of non-professionals, or of professionals of lesser experience, but it also extends to responsibilities in such areas as the formulation and management of budgets and handling external relations with customers and clients on behalf of the organization (Causer and Jones 1996a,b).

As this suggests, a mapping of the relationship between professional and managerial roles and functions is not one which may be adequately attained through the use of a simple dichotomy. Rather, it is necessary to develop a more complex typology which reflects the varying ways in which professional and managerial activities may be related to one another. This typology reflects a continuum of roles rather than discrete categories because different individuals in the same formal position may 'interpret' and 'enact' their roles in different ways. We would suggest that in organizations employing significant numbers of professional employees we can identify three broad roles, each of which may itself be differentiated into two types.

Firstly, there is the role of the *practising (or rank-and-file) professional* – those whose primary function is to engage in the day-to-day exercise of professional activities. Practising professionals may themselves, however, be divided into those whose work involves no supervisory or resource allocation activities (the *pure practitioner*) and those for whom the exercise of such responsibilities is an integral part of their activities, even though they are not formally designated as managers (the *quasi-managerial practitioner*).

Secondly, there are those drawn from the ranks of practising professionals whose primary responsibility is the management of the day-to-day work of other professionals and of the resources utilized in that work – who we may describe as the *managing professional*. However, this group too may display internal differentiation, according to whether or not the managing professional continues, alongside their managerial activity, to maintain some direct engagement in professional practice. The category of 'managing professionals' may therefore be divided into two groups – the *practising managing professional* and the *non-practising managing professional*.

Finally there are those who have an overall managerial responsibility for the activities of professional employees, but are not themselves concerned with the direct management of day-to-day practice. This group, whom we will designate as *general managers*, may, but need not, be drawn from among those with a background in the practice of the profession itself. We can accordingly differentiate within this group between the *professionally grounded general manager* on the one hand, and the *non-professional general manager* on the other.

Of the six groups identified here, five are characterized by their past or present engagement in professional practice, thus emphasizing the complexity of the processes by which professional groups within organizations may be internally stratified. On the one hand, managing professionals (whether continuing to practise or not) and professionally grounded general managers are likely to retain a measure of identification with the professional group, and may well ground their claim to authority in part on this identification. On the other hand, even among practising professionals there will be those whose roles are not those of the pure practitioner, but rather entail undertaking activities of at least a quasi-managerial nature.

The existence of these patterns of internal stratification has significant implications for the nature of professions. To a greater or lesser degree, professional groups have been held together by the notion (or fiction) of equality of competence (Freidson 1994: 142). The undertaking of managerial activities by professionals at various levels of the organization reflects an erosion of this notion, as a key function of these groups may be to monitor (overtly or discreetly) the practice of other professionals, and to institute corrective action where it is deemed necessary. Thus in so far as there *is* a tension between managerial imperatives and professional autonomy, this will commonly be expressed not through the imposition of these imperatives by managers on professionals, but rather through the work of those professionals who engage in managerial or quasi-managerial activities.

A further implication of this internal stratification concerns the nature of professional careers. Where advancement within the profession entails movement into positions which involve control over the work of others, or decisions on the allocation of resources, such movement will be dependent not simply – or even primarily – on the display of professional competence, but also on the possession of what are later described in Chapter 8 (p. 134) as 'managerial assets'. As suggested in that chapter, a distinction may be drawn between the older professions, such as medicine and the law (in which the possession of such assets has traditionally been of restricted significance), and the newer professions embedded in both public and private bureaucracies (where their importance for both professional roles and professional advancement has always been greater). However, it may be argued that recent developments have had the effect of promoting a greater degree of internal stratification within both older and newer professional groups, and hence of enhancing the significance of the possession of managerial assets for members of professional groups in general.

In this chapter we seek to address these issues by examining developments in relation to four groups in three areas – doctors and nurses within the health service, teachers within primary and secondary schools, and social workers within local authority social service departments. While trends towards the 'managerialization' of aspects of professional work in each of these areas have intensified during the 1980s and 1990s, they are not peculiar to this period and need to be situated in their longer-term context.

Historical development of professionals as managers in the public sector

Of the three areas considered here, it is the health service which entails the most complex set of relations between professional and managerial activities. At the creation of the National Health Service the privileged position accorded to the medical profession allowed doctors to undertake de facto managerial functions – particularly as they related to resource allocation – without concomitant managerial accountability (Klein 1989; Harrison and Pollitt 1994: 35; Alaszewski 1995: 60). Despite attempts from the 1960s onwards to bring the implications of medical decisions into the open, the principle of 'clinical autonomy' continued to give doctors a position substantially free from the managerial restraints applied in most organizations (Dent 1993; see Harrison, Chapter 4). The same was not true of other professional groupings within the health service. For these groups, Harrison and Pollitt (1994) argue, the goal of occupational control was most effectively pursued through the creation of their own managerial hierarchies, and an attendant growth in the number and role of managerial professionals. This was effected most notably in nursing, where the implementation of the Salmon Report (1966) led to the creation of an extended nursing management hierarchy. This approach was enhanced by the 1974 NHS reorganization which enshrined the principle of 'consensus management', whereby senior managerial professionals in the nursing hierarchy were integrated into the management team (Harrison and Pollitt 1994: 5–6).

In contrast to the multi-profession NHS, the management of schools – organizations dominated by a single professional group – presents a more clear-cut picture. Although constrained by the policies and procedures of LEAs as well as by statutory requirements, head teachers – drawn exclusively from the teaching profession – enjoyed considerable autonomy over issues of school management and organization (Levačić 1995: 5). The way in which the attendant authority was exercised varied widely, but, for a significant number of heads, the ideal of retaining some element of professional practice alongside their managerial activities constituted a central component of their management style (Hall et al. 1986; Ball 1987: Chs 5 and 6). In terms of our typology many heads adopted the role of the practising managing professional. Prior to the comprehensive reforms of the 1960s, the managing professional role developed below the level of the head to only a limited extent. However, the growth in secondary school size associated with comprehensive reorganization contributed to a situation in which heads of department effectively moved from being senior teachers to becoming middle managers with responsibility for such activities as staff supervision and departmental finance alongside their established teaching role (Dunham 1978; Ribbins 1985). In terms of our typology they shifted increasingly in the direction of the practising managing professional. In contrast, in primary schools –

typically smaller and characterized by generalist rather than subject-divided specialist staff – managerial functions were likely to remain largely concentrated in the head, and even here scope frequently remained for the head to be a teacher who managed rather than a manager who also taught (Levačić 1995: 52).

In social work, as in secondary schools, growth in organizational scale contributed to the growth in managerial professional roles. Prior to the Seebohm Report of 1968 and the subsequent Local Authority Social Services Act of 1970, the fragmentation of social work across a number of institutional settings (local authority child care and welfare departments, hospitals, etc.) limited the growth of managerial hierarchies within the profession, and sustained the existence of supervisory relationships grounded in notions of shared collegial status (Bamford 1982: 49–50). The establishment of unified local authority social services departments led to a rapid proliferation of managerial positions, stratified by function, geographical location or a mixture of the two (Glastonbury et al. 1980: Ch. 5). Those recruited to such positions (and especially to director posts) were drawn largely from the ranks of social workers, although the great majority of those employed by the new departments were typically not social workers but unqualified staff in such areas as domiciliary and residential services (Bamford 1982: 4). Although the appointment of social workers to management posts was intended to link social work values into management, critics from an early stage argued that the new structures were inimical to traditional social work practice and subordinated the judgement of the professional practitioner to increasingly bureaucratized rules and procedures (see Glastonbury et al. 1980; Jones 1996a: 198). The newly appointed directors of social services, although having a background in social work, commonly came to be seen as remote from day-to-day practice by rank-and-file practitioners.

Problems of bureaucratization in social services departments were compounded by the apparently unremitting rise in workloads, as departments found referrals coming from 'an array of state and public authorities which were exploiting the formation of a single agency to off-load their problematic and time-consuming tenants/pupils/patients/claimants/debtors and so forth' (Jones 1996a: 198). At the root of this problem lay the philosophy of the Seebohm Report, which envisaged a generic social work profession serving a wide and somewhat unspecific set of needs. In this situation of rapidly accelerating workloads and attendant increases in staff numbers, the trend to bureaucratization continued, and was reinforced over time by the series of child abuse inquiries which typically gave rise to the development of further reporting and monitoring procedures and an expansion of professional advisory management roles (Glastonbury et al. 1980; Otway 1996).

However, the extent to which this bureaucratization of procedures penetrated the day-to-day practice of social workers is open to question. Pithouse (1987) in a detailed study of the operation of an area office in the early 1980s, suggests that in practice restrictions on the day-to-day autonomy of practitioners were limited. Area managers (general managers in our terms, but still located close to day-to-day practice) played a significant role in seeking to insulate the office from the wider organization. Team leaders, while not engaging directly in practice (and hence non-practising managing professionals in our typology), none the less continued to exercise supervisory roles in a collegial fashion, seeking to remain closely attuned to the practice of team members and to supervise in a way which retained the appearance of equal competence among colleagues.

It is thus clear that trends to an increasing 'managerialization' of certain professional groups were underway well before the advent of the Conservative government in 1979. However, the effect of the public sector reforms introduced over the next 15 years has undoubtedly been to increase the growth of various 'managerial professional' roles and, arguably, to increase the incorporation of managerial elements into the role of rank-and-file practitioners. In the sections which follow we will seek to explore the ways in which this has occurred among the four occupational groups with which we are concerned.

Doctors and management in the NHS

The introduction of general managers into the NHS following the Griffiths Report of 1983 is widely seen as an attempt to overcome the inertia allegedly associated with consensus management and to challenge the vested interests of professional groups within the health service (Klein 1990). With regard to the most powerful of these vested interests, the medical profession, the initiative is widely held to have had a limited effect (see Harrison *et al.* 1992). However, other initiatives may be seen as seeking to incorporate rather than challenge professional groups. Of these, perhaps the most obvious is the incorporation of (hospital and community health service) doctors into management via the system of clinical directorates and the devolution of budgets to clinicians under schemes such as the Resource Management Initiative (Packwood *et al.* 1991; Harrison, Chapter 4). Although the introduction of clinical directorates in certain hospitals pre-dates the NHS reforms of the late 1980s, it has become the principal form of organization in NHS Trusts. Clinical directors, predominantly doctors, manage each directorate, and each trust is required to have a medical director (a doctor) on the Trust board who acts as the ultimate professional authority, overseeing the work of clinical directors among others. The creation of these posts has been seen as a means whereby doctors may be incorporated into the overt processes of decision making within the organization (Harrison and Pollitt 1994: 87–94).

An equally significant development on the purchaser side of the NHS internal market has been the creation of GP fundholding, which has allowed some general practitioners to purchase a range of services and to contract directly with health service providers. Through the independent contractor status that they secured in 1948 (Klein 1990), GPs have long been managers of practice staff (*qua* employers) and practice premises (*qua* business owners) as well as practising clinicians. Although their previously indirect role in service provision has been radically altered by fundholding, there has been a differential impact within and between practices. Fundholding initially attracted few GPs, but it has been estimated that the percentage of GPs who are fundholders increased to 56 per cent by 1997 (Department of Health press release, 96/271). However, not all GPs within a fundholding practice engage with contracting negotiations with providers.

The effect of these processes has been to develop managerial professional roles in a profession where they have hitherto been comparatively underdeveloped. Clinical director and GP fundholder roles clearly entail responsibility for the management of the directorate and practice respectively, including that of medical and other professional staff within it, even though much of the routine administrative work is carried out by non-medical 'business managers'. What is striking here is that, while both clinical directors and GP fundholders have taken on the role of managing professionals, they have done so in ways which emphasize a degree of engagement in continuing professional practice – i.e. they have become practising rather than non-practising managing professionals. In contrast to the majority of professional groups, where career advancement beyond a certain stage has been dependent upon a move away from practice, in medicine (as in law) high status and rewards have been associated with the continuation of practice. Hence, for managing professionals in this area to retain credibility they need to continue in practice.

Such credibility is of particular importance in this case, as it is the management of other medical staff – and in particular other consultants – that has proved particularly problematic for the clinical directorate system (Scrivens 1988; Fitzgerald 1991), although the issue is less of a problem in general practice. The key issue here is not primarily that of resource allocation, but the fraught question of monitoring and controlling work performance. As Harrison and Schultz report in their review of the literature, doctors 'regard overall financial limitations as being legitimate restrictions on their autonomy . . . [but] did not see a legitimate role for peer review or quality assurance' (Harrison and Schultz 1989: 203).

This resistance to peer review and quality assurance is, of course, an expression of the traditional notion of equality of competence and has been expressed through the limitations placed on the development of medical audit. In 1989, the government proposed that medical audit should be voluntary and educational, and that results would be made available to management only in aggregated and anonymized form. This was indicative of a concern not to trespass on the work performance aspect of medical autonomy. However, Pollitt (1993) has indicated how the audit process may be developed in ways which raise issues of individual accountability. Whereas purchasers previously relied on cost and activity data by which to assess services, their formal involvement in audit since 1994 has given them an opportunity to assess the clinical performance of services. Although the resultant data remains somewhat equivocal (Exworthy 1995), this has the potential to create a situation in which failure to ameliorate apparently inadequate performance may adversely affect the organization's position in the internal market. Consequently Trust managers (including, critically, medical and clinical directors) may need to identify and act upon what are seen as inadequate levels of performance (Harrison and Pollitt 1994: 104).

Recent trends in contracting are likely to reinforce these processes. Although many initial contracts were formulated only between managers, subsequent rounds of contracting have sought progressively to involve clinicians. Many NHS contracts are now placed with clinical directorates within a provider, involving a selective range of individuals, including clinical directors. As a result, these managing professionals are implicated yet more firmly into the management of the organization and committed to executing the contract, a process which will necessarily involve some managerial direction of other professionals.

Harrison (Chapter 4) suggests that recent trends in contracting may represent the beginning of a shift in the locus of medical autonomy away from consultants to GPs. The development of 'total fundholding', allowing GPs (usually organized in consortia) to purchase virtually all forms of secondary and tertiary care, represents a significant increase in GP autonomy, even compared to standard fundholding. Fundholding also reinforces the role of the managing professional on the purchaser side of the health market. The initial development of fundholding has already precipitated a division of labour within practices, with one or two GPs (usually in mid-career) taking primary responsibility for the managerial aspects of the process. These tendencies will be taken further with the development of consortia for, as Harrison points out, 'amongst a consortium of thirty or forty GP principals, a de facto managerial hierarchy seems bound to emerge' (Chapter 4: 58).

The growth of the managing professional role within medicine (in both primary and secondary care) therefore seems indisputable, although as we have seen, this has largely taken the form of the development of the practising managing professional rather than of the managing professional entirely divorced from day-to-day practice. It is the precise significance of this growth which is open to debate. On the one hand, the involvement of medical staff in formal management structures and processes may be seen as a way of incorporating these professionals whose position was previously difficult to challenge. As Hoggett (1994: 43) puts it (writing of the public sector more generally): 'rather than try to control professionals by managers, you convert professionals into managers (by giving them budgets or by setting them adrift as quasi-autonomous business units)'.

On the other hand, this may be seen as a process whereby professional control is reasserted (Lukes 1974). Hunter (1992), for example, suggests that the emergence of the 'doctor-manager' embodies the possibility of the medical profession capturing the management agenda, thereby making it more difficult for managerial challenges to their autonomy. The reality perhaps lies somewhere between these two positions. Given the strength and status of medicine as an occupation, it seems improbable that doctors entering into managerial roles will completely abandon their traditional occupational commitments and outlooks, and this is likely to be reinforced by continuing engagement in practice at some level. At the same time, the operation of competitive pressures and the need to secure contracts may push some doctors in an increasingly managerial direction. In particular, the combination of market pressures and accountability to purchasers has the potential to lead to an erosion of the notion of equal competence, and the evolution of the managing professional role into one which increasingly entails control over the work of other professionals.

Whatever the outcomes of these processes, it is important to note that, in at least one respect, the growth of the managing professional role clearly represents an assertion of continuing medical dominance. Although clinical directors will ultimately be accountable to a general manager in the wider organization, *within* their directorate, they will have ultimate authority and responsibility for the work of *all* occupational groups. In this way the primacy of the medical profession within the interprofessional division of labour is maintained, and arguably enhanced.

Nursing and management

While the introduction of general management into the NHS had a limited effect on the medical profession, it impacted significantly on other professional groups. As we have noted earlier, such groups had sought to secure occupational control through the creation of their own management hierarchies as part of nursing's professionalization strategy (Witz 1992: Walby and Greenwell 1994). The introduction of general management posed significant challenges to these hierarchies.

At one level the work of fully qualified nurses has long involved engagement in functions of a managerial kind, with both staff nurses and sisters/charge nurses having significant responsibilities for the direction and monitoring of the work of junior and unqualified nursing staff (Mackay 1993: 38–9). Sisters and charge nurses, in particular, have performed roles which are close to those of our managing professional model, but typically with the retention of at least an element of practice.

Advancing beyond ward level entailed a shift away from professional practice into more of a general manager role. However, given the existence of professionally based hierarchies, such general manager roles remained grounded in the profession and entailed continuing identification with it. With the introduction of general managers without such a professional grounding, challenges could be mounted to the established professional hierarchy, and nursing lost its automatic right of representation on higher level decision-making bodies (Walby *et al.* 1994: 141–3). While subsequent developments may have seen some reversal of these processes, with nurses being represented on some NHS Trust boards (either directly as representatives of nursing or in an associated professional capacity), and some movement of nurses into senior management positions (NHS Management Executive 1993), the scope for managerial development within nursing remains restricted. The nursing officer/nurse manager role, acting as a link between nursing staff and the director of nursing services, has been substantially eroded in recent years, a process likely to be taken further by the establishment of clinical directorates (Mackay 1993: 251).

The same processes which may be seen as eroding the role and number of nurse managers have at the same time led to an increasing definition of the role of ward sisters in managerial terms. Although the extent of budgetary devolution remains variable, nursing sisters are increasingly being seen as ward managers, with enhanced responsibility for control over the utilization of budgets, but limited influence over their level (Alaszewski 1995: 65). One possible effect of these changes is an increasing shift in the activity of sisters towards the non-practising managing professional role, although this may be offset by tendencies to the devolution of management-type responsibilities to those lower in the nursing hierarchy and the increasing division between registered nurses and NVQ-qualified health care assistants. As Walby *et al.* point out, it is registered nurses who control the training and assessment of health care assistants, and who direct their work (Walby *et al.* 1994: 138). While this formalized division of the nursing labour force into a 'core' and 'periphery' may be seen as a response to market pressures to develop a more cost-effective skill mix in the ward setting, it also reflects the professionalization strategy pursued by leading figures in the nursing profession over the last decade. Centring around the Project 2000 initiative, this has shifted the training of the nursing elite away from the hospital setting into colleges and universities, thereby establishing nursing at its higher levels as a graduate profession. A key facet of this has been the attempt to establish a distinctive knowledge base for nursing, with an associated stress on the role of the qualified nurse in the management of patient care. The effect is thus to reinforce the role of the qualified nurse as a managing professional, albeit with elements of a continuing involvement in practice.

Recent developments in nursing therefore present a somewhat paradoxical picture. On the one hand, developments initiated from within the profession itself, as well as general trends to budgetary devolution, have encouraged an increasing managerialization of aspects of the nursing role, at least in the upper echelons. On the other hand, the erosion of the nurse manager role has placed increasing constraints on movement from the managing professional role on the ward to a professionally grounded general manager role beyond the confines of the ward setting.

Management in schools

In examining the changing role of the managerial professional in teaching, four factors may be seen as having had a particular effect: the introduction of local management of schools (LMS); the introduction of a more public system of accountability through regular inspections; the introduction of the National Curriculum; and the introduction of a 'quasi-market' through open enrolment and formula funding that links school budgets directly to pupil numbers.

Under local management of schools (LMS) an increasing proportion of the education budget has been devolved from LEAs to schools. At the same time, responsibilities for budgets and staffing decisions have been placed formally in the hands of school governors, although in practice heads may substantially exercise these powers on their behalf (Levačić 1995: 136). The most immediately apparent effect of this has been to enhance still further the existing managerial role of heads in secondary schools, and to push primary heads increasingly in this direction also. For many heads, managing the budget and associated activities has become increasingly time-consuming, while the enhanced powers (at least in principle) of governors have increased the need for heads to manage their relations with this group (Evetts 1993; Levačić 1995: 136).

In this situation it has become increasingly difficult for heads to maintain the role of a practising managing professional, and even the maintenance of this role in its non-practising form may become increasingly problematic, with heads moving in the direction of a professionally grounded general manager role. In both secondary and primary schools there has been some tendency for heads to become increasingly involved in budgetary matters and to delegate the traditional role of instructional leadership to deputies (Bowe and Ball 1992; Maw 1994; Maychell 1994). Within the school, LMS may lead to more formalized procedures of resource allocation, with bidding by departments linked to curriculum development plans (Levačić 1995: 98). Such trends will emphasize further the managerial aspects of the role of the departmental head, and the increasing importance of managerial skills in the performance of that role. Departmental heads may become increasingly pushed in the direction of the managing professional model, although with a continuing involvement in professional practice.

The introduction of the National Curriculum and national testing at selected ages arguably reinforces these processes. As organizational success comes to be measured at least partly in terms of test results, so the managerial accountability of departmental heads for those teachers in their departments will tend to increase, as will the emphasis on formalized curriculum planning. In this situation traditional assumptions of equality of competence come under increasing pressure, and the role of the head of department as manager is further emphasized.

The tendency to increased formal planning is reinforced by the system of inspections carried out under the auspices of the Office for Standards in Education (Ofsted). While focused significantly on actual professional practice in the classroom, such inspections also place heavy emphasis upon the formulation and implementation of development and action plans, and the quality of curriculum, pastoral and financial management within the institution. The impetus towards the development of more formalized plans and procedures, and the institution of systems for the monitoring of performance outcomes, may thus be seen as reinforcing the importance for teachers of developing management-type skills for the performance of their activities and, in particular, for their career advancement.

The introduction of systematic Ofsted inspections was designed as a means of remedying what was seen as one of the barriers to parental choice of schools, namely the absence of adequate information on the part of prospective and actual consumers in the education market (compare the role of medical audit in the NHS). This relates to the attempt to create greater responsiveness on the part of schools by linking funding to pupil numbers and abolishing the right of schools and LEAs to limit entry below the school's maximum capacity ('open enrolment'). The extent to which this has actually created a competitive environment is open to question (Levačić 1995: 103; Woods *et al.* 1996), but it is clear that the new environment has pushed schools in the direction of greater promotional activities than hitherto. Again this has required the development of new roles and the acquisition of new skills, and has reinforced the managerial components of the work of more senior teaching staff.

The overall effect of the changes in education over the last decade has thus been both to enhance the established managerial components of existing roles, from heads down through deputies to heads of departments, and to increase the importance of managerial-cum-administrative activities for teachers more generally. However, these tendencies have a complex relationship with professional roles and philosophies. Some writers (for example Bowe and Ball 1992) have seen LMS as giving rise to a growing gulf between the head, on the one hand, and rank-and-file teachers on the other. It should however be remembered that even prior to reform, heads could be remote figures operating at some distance from their staff. What is striking is the way in which managerial functions may continue to be exercised in ways which reflect a 'professional' rather than an 'entrepreneurial' orientation. One example of this is the way in which secondary schools have frequently reacted to open enrolment and formula funding. In their detailed study of 11 secondary schools, Woods *et al.* found that while schools *were* engaged in a range of promotional activities, the primary emphasis was placed upon developing close relationships with feeder schools, rather than seeking to 'market research' parental preferences and respond directly to these. They comment that 'part of the explanation for this is likely to be an inherent professional reluctance to be led by "consumers" rather than driven by the profession's own expertise' (Woods *et al.* 1996: 23). The establishment of links with other educational institutions is, they argue, much less problematic for schools than dealing with an amorphous mass of parents – to which one may add that this is especially the case where those institutions are themselves staffed and managed by members of the same profession. (In the case of primary schools, there is less scope for this form of 'vertical integration', and it is here that promotional activities directed at parents are likely to have greatest significance; see Menter and Muschamp, Chapter 5).

Similar considerations may be applied to other aspects of the management of schools. While LMS has undoubtedly led to a greater formalization of budgetary and allocative procedures, Levačić notes that in many other areas (for example decisions on class sizes, mixed-year teaching and amount of non-contact time for teachers), traditional patterns of professional judgement continue to prevail.

> There was no hard evidence that the chosen way of using resources was more effective or efficient in terms of pupils' learning than alternatives which had not been considered or had been considered and rejected. Nor did schools appear to undertake any formal or systematic evaluation of the resulting outcomes of these decisions. They were evaluated, in so far as they were, through intuition and judgement.
>
> (Levačić 1995: 151)

Intuition and judgement are, of course, hallmarks of professional discretion. Furthermore, even where financial factors *do* impact directly on decisions about school organization, these are not necessarily imposed by managerial professionals. Thus in one of the schools studied by Huckman and Fletcher, the decision to respond to staff cuts by a reintroduction of streaming appeared to emanate primarily from the staff, who felt that it would be easier to cope with larger classes by the abandonment of mixed-ability teaching (Huckman and Fletcher 1996: 144).

On the face of it, a decision to opt out of local authority control and become grant maintained (GM) might be seen as the clearest expression of a desire on the part of a school's senior staff to enter into entrepreneurial competition. Opting out, while undertaken by only a minority of schools, has been heavily concentrated in the secondary sector: some 16

per cent of such schools in England and Wales have become grant maintained, compared with only 2 per cent of primary schools (Power *et al.*
1996: 106). We may speculate that this difference partly reflects the
greater pre-existing development of management roles and structures in
secondary schools, and hence a greater perceived capacity to deal with
the demands of GM status. At the same time, decisions to opt out have
been driven by a variety of factors, not least the financial incentives
attached to doing so (Fitz *et al.* 1993).

Moreover, it is by no means clear that opting out embodies a radically
different approach to school management than that entailed by local
management within local authority control. Far from seeking to pioneer
curricular innovation, the option of securing business support as a route
to becoming technology colleges is one which has been pursued by only
a small minority of opted-out schools. While GM schools have sought to
market themselves to parents in ways not dissimilar to those employed
by other schools, they have tended to do so through an emphasis on the
maintenance of 'traditional' educational values (Fitz *et al.* 1993).
Whether this should be seen as an astute marketing ploy or as the seizing
of an opportunity to reassert a significant indigenous strand of professional ideology is a matter of interpretation.

The managerialization of social work

In the second section, 'Historical development of professionals as managers in the public sector', we noted the way in which, in the years following their inception, local authority social services departments
became the repository for dealing with a diverse range of individual and
social problems. One striking feature of the changes to social work insti-
tuted in the early 1990s was the abandonment of the Seebohm model of
a wide-ranging social work service and a de facto restriction of the client
base to 'the vulnerable and dependent who need special protection, in
particular children who are at risk, people with learning difficulties, physical disabilities and mental illness, and certain groups of elderly people'
(Alaszewski 1995: 68). The role of social workers in relation to these
groups has also been increasingly defined in a new way, stressing the role
of managerial or quasi-managerial activities. As in the NHS, the introduction of a purchaser–provider split – particularly in the area of community care – is designed to secure a cost-effective use of resources
through the use of a professionally informed purchaser allocating
resources to buy, for example, domiciliary support or residential care on
behalf of the client. While this 'care manager' role is not one which
necessarily needs to be undertaken by a social worker, 'their professional
role in social services departments, the lead public agency involved
in implementing community care policy, will always make them a
major contributor to care management where it is undertaken by

multi-disciplinary teams or by people whose background is in other professional areas' (Payne 1995: 5). At the same time, the care manager role – by whomsoever it is undertaken – clearly embodies a significant ambiguity, which on the face of it has scope for generating tension between social work practitioners and their managers. On the one hand the care manager is charged with assessing clients' needs and ensuring that these are met through the package of services purchased. But, on the other, they are accountable to managers for ensuring that the resources available are rationed so as to remain within the available budget – an accountability arguably reinforced by the House of Lords decision (March 1997) establishing the legality of rationing the availability of services in the light of budgetary constraints. Furthermore, care managers may have limited control in practice as to what services are purchased or in ensuring the maintenance of service quality (Langan and Clarke 1994: 84–90).

The position in respect of the other primary area of social services departments' work – child care – shows parallel developments. As Otway (1996) indicates, there has been a steady shift since the 1960s away from seeing child abuse primarily as a medico-social problem requiring therapeutic intervention with the family, to a perspective which sees it primarily as a socio-legal problem in which the main emphasis is placed upon investigation and assessment of the evidence, and in which social workers increasingly act as part of the legal system. This has generated an increasingly rule-governed approach to the handling of such cases, sparked not only by the failure of social services departments effectively to protect abused children in certain highly publicized cases, but also by concerns at the potential abuse of parental rights and interests in others. More generally, the handling of child welfare issues too is now cast in what are effectively 'care management' terms, with the local authority having a duty to meet the needs of children in their care through the assembly of care packages. While the local authority may continue to provide such services as day care and accommodation, increasing emphasis is laid upon partnerships with the voluntary sector and other providers.

The upshot of these changes is what Alaszewski (1995: 72) describes as 'a radical restructuring of social work', with a concomitant change in the role of social workers. It is not simply that social workers 'will experience greater accountability to managers' (Alaszewski 1995: 72) for their use of resources, but that their role will itself become increasingly managerial in nature. As Langan and Clarke point out, to be effective the care management role requires high levels of training and expertise in such areas as budget management and contract negotiations. As a consequence the role of the social worker will become increasingly that of the quasi-managerial practitioner, with managerial skills and functions becoming an integral part of the professional role. This is something which has already been reflected in the training of social workers, with its increasing emphasis on 'competences' in place of more traditional academic concerns (Ford 1996; see also Jones 1996a; Webb 1996).

On the most extreme interpretation, these trends may be seen as signalling the end of social work as a distinct activity, as child protection, community care and family service functions are fragmented into different parts of the social services department, and the role of those engaged in them is focused increasingly on the purchaser function (Clarke 1996: 55–8). This scenario is, as Clarke concedes, 'rather apocalyptic'. Traditional social work skills are likely to continue to play a central role in, for example, processes of need and risk assessment, and although social work functions may become fragmented, the pre-Seebohm experience indicates that fragmentation is not in itself incompatible with the notion of a common occupation.

It is, however, clear that present trends in social work are pushing the occupation itself in a direction where the acquisition of managerial skills will become increasingly important for both the exercise of social work roles and for longer-term career progression. These tendencies contain the potential to develop tensions between social work practitioners and those with formal managerial responsibilities. As noted above, general managers at area level may have acted to insulate practitioners from the demands of the wider organization, and team leaders have operated in ways which stress a common identity and competence as social workers. The more emphasis is placed on the management of resources as a key facet of the social work role, the more team leaders, as non-practising managing professionals, are likely to find themselves exercising direct control and overt monitoring of their subordinates' actions. At the same time, however, it may be suggested that the more social work functions come to be defined in what are substantially managerial terms, the more this potential for conflict is likely to be mitigated.

Conclusions

In this chapter we have sought to delineate the changing role of professionals in management in three areas of the public sector. The overall pattern is clear. There is a general tendency for the managerial component of established managerial professional roles to increase, and for managerial components to become an increasingly important part of the work roles of most professional groups. However, there are significant variations.

It may be argued that the greatest change is that found in the medical profession. Although some doctors have long had an involvement in management, movement into formal management positions or taking on broader managerial responsibilities has not formed part of the typical medical career. Most doctors have remained practitioners throughout their career, and have been able to secure high status and rewards by doing so. In this respect the medical profession has been atypical, and has been able to retain this position partly because, from the inception of the NHS, doctors have secured (and the state has been prepared to concede) certain of the privileges of employment without concomitant subordination to managerial control. The increasing integration of some doctors into formalized management structures (in a way which has long been common in other professional settings) thus represents an important change, with the development of a significant managing professional role in both Trust hospitals and fundholding practices. The future development of these roles within medicine may depend on the fate of the NHS reforms, but pressures for greater accountability and for control over NHS expenditure are unlikely to abate. In this situation it seems probable that the incorporation of doctors into management will continue as a means of enhancing the control of professional work in ways which are already manifest in other areas. To what extent this represents control *of* the profession and to what extent control *by* the profession is debatable, and the question itself reflects the ambiguity of the role of the managerial professional.

In the other three areas we have examined, career advancement, at least beyond a certain point, has long entailed movement away from practice into a role which is either predominantly managerial in nature or at least involves some combination of management and continuing practice. The trends we have considered in this chapter will, in general, have had the effect of reinforcing this process. This development is perhaps clearest in teaching, where government reforms have shifted the work of those in both the middle ranks and at the top of the school hierarchy in the direction of managerial and administrative tasks. Again, it seems unlikely that developments in the foreseeable future will lead to a significant reversal of this trend. Indeed, processes such as external monitoring and accountability are likely if anything to intensify.

In social work, too, career advancement is likely to become increasingly dependent upon the possession of managerial skills and assets. The increased emphasis on care management will demand such skills from social workers and place managers and supervisors in a situation where their role is increasingly defined in terms of managing and deploying resources. The process of a managerialization of social work activities, initially set in train by the implementation of the Seebohm proposals in the 1970s, will continue.

In nursing, we also see evidence of an increasingly managerial definition of professional work, at least so far as the upper echelon of fully qualified nursing staff are concerned. The division between registered nurses and health care assistants, reinforced by the Project 2000 changes in nurse education, is likely to locate the work of nurses increasingly in the management of patient care and in the overview of the work of those who provide the more basic practical aspects of that care. As this case suggests, the managerialization of aspects of professional work should not necessarily be seen as undermining professional status, but may also serve as a means of enhancing it. However, the erosion of the nursing hierarchy above ward level may impair the scope for movement into more general management roles.

As these examples indicate, the relationship between professional and managerial activities – always more complex than the simple thesis of professional–management conflict implied – has become if anything more complex over time. Processes of marketization and pressures for increased accountability have tended to erode traditional notions of equality of competence on the part of professional employees, and have set up pressures to render professional performance more open to scrutiny. But the very fact that performance of professional tasks rests upon the possession of specialist knowledge or expertise means that those drawn from the ranks of the profession are likely to play a central role in this process (Boreham 1983). Thus what from one perspective may be seen as a process of managerial control, from another may be seen as a means of retaining a measure of professional self-regulation. Professions are likely to be increasingly characterized by processes of internal stratification, in which both professional identities and sources of authority become more ambiguous in nature. The intra-organizational divisions on which we have focused in this chapter will be compounded by inter-organizational divisions, both those fostered by the development of quasi-market competition and those based on the growth of external regulation. The growing use of external inspection and audit in a number of areas itself draws upon the expertise of those with professional backgrounds and experience to monitor performance within the areas of professional competence.

In this situation, the status and power of professions may come increasingly to depend upon their ability to cast their goals and objectives in appropriate terms. As we have indicated, the development of a more explicitly managerial definition of the role of the qualified nurse can be seen as part of a strategy to enhance the status of the professional group, and it is not difficult to envisage similar developments in other areas. While 'care management' has been viewed with trepidation by many social workers, one can see how the redefinition of social work in the language of care management could provide a basis for claiming a specialist expertise and an associated professional jurisdiction in the face of threatened encroachment by other occupational groups. Likewise, the increasing involvement of doctors in management may provide scope for the casting of medical goals in the language of markets and competition. In these circumstances managerial and professional discourses are likely to become increasingly fused.

Notwithstanding the interprofessional and intersectoral variations described in this chapter, it is clear that the boundaries between professional and managerial work in the public sector are becoming increasingly blurred. The notion of a clear-cut division between managers and professionals – or even between managerial and rank-and-file professionals – is in some respects increasingly unhelpful. Not only will it become increasingly difficult to classify the *functions* of an activity through a simple dichotomy, but comparable problems will also arise in the analysis of the *identities* of those occupying such positions (see Halford and Leonard, Chapter 7).

These conclusions suggest that managerial assets are becoming of increasing importance for career advancement within the professions. To some extent, such assets have always been important in most professions, but their significance is intensifying. For many people engaged in professional activity it may become increasingly inappropriate to ask whether they are a professional *or* a manager, for the essential nature of their work will lie in the combination of both elements.

7 | New identities? Professionalism, managerialism and the construction of self

Susan Halford and Pauline Leonard

Introduction

This book has provided many examples of the numerous ways in which the roles and tasks of professionals working in education, health and social services have been reshaped by a 'creeping managerialism' (Coyle 1988) pervading the public sector in recent years. This has entailed not only the introduction of newly created and newly defined management posts, but the redistribution of managerial responsibilities across the professional hierarchy. In schools and hospitals up and down the country, heads of French departments and sisters of maternity wards alike now have budgets to manage and staffing decisions to make, in addition to judging the merits of exam boards, or post-natal care and other issues integral to their profession. Clearly, the jobs of professionals are changing. But so too is the 'business' of management, as the nature of 'good' management is redefined, and the emphasis placed on new skills and competencies. (See Chapter 1 for a detailed discussion.)

Our key concern in this chapter is how people occupying these professional and managerial posts respond to the changes that are reshaping their jobs, particularly to the spread of managerial responsibilities and new managerial discourses. We know that the *content* of work in the restructured public sector is changing (Halford *et al.* 1997), but how has this affected employees *personally*, in terms of their identities or senses of self? Has the broadening definition of what it is to be a teacher, or a doctor, or a social worker, resulted in changes to the way people see and feel about themselves, a shifting in the construction of who they are? Any answer to this question depends largely on the way in which the relationship between work and identity is understood. Two conceptions of this relationship have dominated the literature on work. On the one hand, work is thought to determine identity, so that 'who we are' is constructed out of 'what we do'. On the other hand, individual, innate, preformed identities are seen to determine the way in which work is carried out, so that 'what we do' is constructed out of 'who we are'. Thus, depending on which school of thought is pursued, the answer to our question seems to be either that people's identities will change dramatically following public sector restructuring, or that they will change very little, as individuals' stable, inner core resists situational change.

In fact, much of the literature on restructuring in the public sector falls into the former camp, suggesting that 'new managerialism' has indeed constructed new forms of identity which have been adopted by public sector staff (for example Leach *et al.* 1994; Miller 1994; du Gay 1996a). However, a closer examination of some of the individual accounts of public sector workers seems to problematize this analysis. In this chapter we make this point using, first, accounts offered by teachers of the relationships between their work, the restructuring of education and their sense of self; second, we draw on accounts offered by managers more generally. These reveal that identities cannot merely be 'read off' from a given context, but take many forms, and may encompass individual practices of modification and resistance. This finding endorses some of the central points made in contemporary work on identity and subjectivity within social theory more generally. In the final part of this chapter we turn to this literature in order to challenge some of the prevailing assumptions about work and identity, and to suggest some new ways of understanding how employees of public sector organizations are responding to recent organizational changes.

Work and identity: which way round?

There have been two main ways of thinking about the relationship between work and identity. The first approach has dominated industrial and economic sociology. Here it is widely assumed that individual identities are largely determined by work roles. This may be as a consequence of an *external* imposition of identity, whereby employing organizations bend individual aspirations, values and identities into line with organizational goals and priorities. Alternatively, or even as part of the same process, the work-based construction of personal identity may be seen as the outcome of *internal* processes, specifically the pursuit of personal self-interest. This argument suggests that individuals take on certain identities in order to maximize returns to themselves, particularly in terms of income and status. This may begin as a conscious process but, over time, identities become internalized in the sub-conscious. Thus, identity is etched onto individuals as they fill certain occupational slots. While personal choice may play some initial role in the choice of occupation, from that point onwards individuals develop distinctive identities as a consequence of their *structural* location.

The second approach has been popular in organizational sociology and management studies. Inspired by more 'romantic' visions of human nature, these analyses draw on the assumption that each person has a 'deep interior' (Gergen 1992: 209). Each and everyone of us is a unique and different individual, with an inner repository of highly individual capacities and characteristics – in short, a *soul*. Organizational theories which follow this argument claim that it behoves organizations to enable and empower individuals to 'be themselves' (Evans and Russell 1989; Morgan 1993): to express themselves fully and creatively, to fulfil all their needs and motivations, so that true 'excellence' will emerge (for example Peters and Waterman 1982). Here, work is an *agentic* activity, a way of expressing true identity.

Both these approaches, the structural and the agentic, infuse the literature on 'managerialism' and 'professionalism'. However, an assumption common to *both* lines of analysis is that 'managers' and 'professionals' are distinctive people; that the individuals filling either slot possess quite different identities. Typically, while 'the professional' is altruistic, independent and creative, 'the manager' is self-interested, conventional and conformist. (See Chapter 1 for a more detailed discussion.)

The conformity of 'the manager' is explained as a result of embeddedness in the routines of bureaucratic life. Indeed, Merton (1957) argued that bureaucracies *depended* ultimately 'upon infusing group participants with appropriate structures and sentiments' (p. 199) and that there were 'definite arrangements in the bureaucracy for inculcating and reinforcing these sentiments' (p. 199). Thus according to Merton, bureaucratic rules and regulations ensure a conformity which is internalized through the inducements offered by career structures, incremental salaries, pensions and so on: ' [t]he official is tacitly expected to and largely does adapt his [*sic*] thoughts, feelings and actions to the prospect of this career' (pp. 200–1). This managerial identity is often thought to extend beyond the confines of the workplace. Following Whyte (1957), Savage *et al.* (1992) claim that the managerial identity leads to specific patterns of 'inconspicuous consumption', typically in the suburbs, where the priority is 'not to break ranks with the group norms and cultural practices of the area in question' (Savage *et al.* 1992: 102). Utilizing Bourdieu's (1990) conceptualization of taste as an 'endless battle to assert identities, social positions and worth' (Savage *et al.* 1992: 100), Savage *et al.* go on to analyse extensive information on the consumption habits of over 5000 Britons, and conclude that managers' lifestyle choices today remain staid and conventional, especially compared with those of professionals.

In contrast to this structural analysis of managers, Vinnicombe (1987) suggests that the key determinant of managers' character is their individual personalities. Vinnicombe describes four different types of managers: the Traditionalist (practical, sensible, reliable, systematic, dependable, realistic, etc.); the Catalyst (charismatic, caring, enthusiastic, good with people, flexible); the Visionary (intellectual, creative, progressive, outspoken, good at decision making and problem solving); and the Troubleshooter/Negotiator (pragmatic, problem solving, responsive, perceptive, knowledgeable). Each personality has a valuable role to play in organizational management, but the different personalities need to be recognized, appreciated and exploited if they are to be used effectively (Bates and Kiersey 1984). Similar points are made in research which emphasizes the different identities – and therefore skills and abilities – which women and men are thought to bring to organizational life, and especially to management roles (see Leonard 1995 for a review; also Ferguson 1984; Marshall 1984; Hegelson 1990; Rosener 1990; Ozga 1993). These studies reinforce the assumption that it is pre-existing identity which is the primary determinant of how work is done, rather than the content of the work role itself.

Turning to the literature on 'professionals', a similar division in approach can be detected. On the one hand, much of the literature assumes that professionals *develop* distinctive identities as a consequence of their occupation. For example, Friedson (1994) suggests three aspects to the construction of shared identity among those belonging to the same profession. At least, he argues, the career prospects associated with professional qualification lead to commitment and identification on self-interested economic grounds. Further, the shared experience of long and rigorous training 'does not merely insert "knowledge" into people's heads, but also builds expectations and commitments . . . specialised occupational identities get constructed' (p. 99). Finally, a professional lifetime spent doing the same tasks as a group of peers leads to 'identification with their occupation, their occupational co-workers and their work' (p. 123). In fact, according to Friedson, the existence of shared professional identity is a key criterion for arguing that a 'profession' exists at all. (See Chapter 1 for further discussion of this point.) However, while Friedson (1994) provides general grounds for expecting to find coherent professional identities, these do not tell us much about their actual content. Across the professions, this content is marked in no small part by distinctions from the bureaucrat. Professionals, it is assumed, are not tied to particular organizations for their careers but retain an extra-organizational independence. Their identities are linked to particular bodies of knowledge and expertise and not to bureaucratic procedures, organizational politics or even to interpersonal (management) skills. But, of course, this depends on *which* profession we are talking about. Jones (see Chapter 3) characterizes a highly specific identity associated with the professional social worker; this contrasts dramatically with, say, the professional identity of doctors or teachers. Thus specific identities tend to be attached to both professions as a whole and to particular professional groups.

In contrast to this, other studies start from the view that people have distinctive and well-formed identities which they take with them as they enter the professions. Researchers in the field of education have shown how individual teachers exhibit marked individuality, displaying 'important distinctions in attitude, performance and strategies' (Goodson 1981: 69). Goodson focuses on teachers' 'lives outside school, their latent identities and cultures' (p. 69), all of which, he believes, have an important impact on their work as teachers. Similarly Beynon argues that '[t]eachers are not . . . cardboard cut-outs: behind their teaching lies a range of motives and emotions . . . they are influenced by past, as well as contemporary, events' (Beynon 1985: 13). Beynon shows that teachers bring different 'historical loyalties, values, educational goals and self-images' with them to schools. Other research has supported this view, and demonstrated that people seek out particular workplaces (not just occupations) where they feel they can 'be themselves' or 'express themselves'. For example, Nias (1985, 1989) provides accounts of the ways in which primary teachers' initial idealism can be maintained, by seeking out – even by moving school if necessary – like-minded teachers to reinforce their own strongly held beliefs and conceptions of the work of teaching. Thus the key thrust of the work in this area is that, although there are pressures to adapt and develop self identity within professions such as teaching, considerable attention should also be given to identities already established in life outside the workplace and consequently to differences between members of the same profession.

In sum, when thinking about the relationship between work and identity, we have seen that persuasive evidence exists on both sides of the structure–agency dichotomy. How does each of these perspectives stand up in the light of the dramatic changes which have reshaped the public sector over the past 15 years? To what extent does fundamental organizational restructuring, and changes to professional roles and meanings, impact on identity at work? The question therefore is: to what extent have these specific changes in the public sector impacted on the construction of self?

New identities? Recent changes in the public sector and the construction of self

As Chapter 1 showed, recent initiatives aimed at changing the public sector contain embedded critiques of both traditional professional and traditional managerial identities. But what implications do these macro-level changes have for the construction of individual identities? How do individuals embedded in traditional conceptions of 'the professional' or 'the manager' – whether understood as the outcome of structural or agentic processes – relate to the shifting fortunes of these categories? Do individual self-concepts shift in relation to broader discursive changes?

These questions have been partially addressed in some of the broader analyses of contemporary public sector change and by more recent theoretical accounts of the relationship between the new managerialism and self-identity. Indeed, several writers suggest that recent reforms in the public sector have been *precisely about* changing the identities of public sector professionals and managers. du Gay (1996b) argues that the Conservative government's reforms of the public sector during the 1980s were, at a general level, a cultural crusade 'concerned with the attitudes, values and forms of self-understanding embedded in both individual and institutional activities' (p. 151). Similarly, Leach *et al.* (1994) argue that the specific reforms to local government constituted 'a revolution in organizational self-image and behaviour' (p. 73). Such revolutions cannot take place in the abstract, independently of the individuals who constitute organizational image and behaviour. Indeed, the accomplishment of change in the public sector (or in any organization for that matter) depends, in part, on the identification of staff with the new values and priorities. In other words, change will only take place if individuals 'live out' or 'embody' new practices (Halford and Savage 1995).

Exploring this line of argument both Miller (1992, 1994) and du Gay (1996a,b) trace the links between new managerial discourses and the reconstruction of individual identities. Miller focuses on the ascendancy of accounting practice within managerial discourse. He suggests that this shift has been particularly profound within the public sector where 'the notion of good management . . . has become synonymous with "management by accounting"' (1994: 24). (See also Tongue 1993.) In turn, Miller claims, accountancy practice has profound implications for the self-construction of public sector managers. The conceptual link lies in Miller's understanding of accountancy as a 'practice of government' (Miller 1994: 63), which seeks 'to align socio-political objectives with the activities and relations of individuals' (Miller and Rose 1988: 171). Accountancy 'acts upon the conduct of individuals' (p. 171) by offering a particular set of possibilities for the constitution of selfhood. At the core of accountancy lies *calculation*, and calculation is predicated on the existence of regular, predictable and essentially calculable behaviours. With the ascendancy of accountancy practice, individuals become both *subject to* its demands (externally regulated or controlled by calculations made elsewhere) and also *subjects of* accountancy practice (individually committed to evaluating their own activities and those of others through the calculative routines of accountancy). To become subjects of accountancy practice is made all the more attractive by the apparently exponential rise in the status of accountancy throughout the twentieth century, and its particular ascendancy in the public sector over the past decade (Miller 1992). Indeed, Miller claims, '[t]he calculative technologies of accountancy hold out the promise that one can transform all individuals, whether they be managers, workers, doctors, or teachers into calculating selves' (p. 70).

Confirming the empirical salience of Miller's argument, Walby and Greenwell's (1994) account of recent changes in the NHS suggests that doctors are being turned into managers via the devolution of financial responsibility. Doctors' increasingly overt involvement in financial allocation is seen as part of their 'managerialization' (p. 60). Furthermore, doctors themselves have initiated the practice of 'medical audit', implementing the language of accountancy in the transformation of the NHS.

The extensive claims made for 'accountancy' are echoed by du Gay (1996a,b,c) in his arguments about 'enterprise'. 'Enterprise', he argues, lies at the heart of recent changes in the government of organizational life and has, in turn, impacted on the construction of both organizational and personal identities. The 'enterprise culture' emphasizes energy, initiative, self-reliance and personal responsibility, encouraging the creation of 'autonomous, productive, self-regulating individuals' (1996a: 60). These qualities are understood to be desirable for organizations so that they may survive in an increasingly complex globalizing context, but also for individuals, who 'come to identify themselves and conceive of their interests in terms of these new words and images' (p. 53). This transference of organizational priorities into individual priorities, embedded in individual identities, takes place through mechanisms which du Gay refers to as 'technologies of government' (for example the use of 'strategy' as a way of organizing language and thought, and the deliberate development and deployment of specific values through organizational cultures). Through these technologies, organizational and individual objectives merge. Thus du Gay emphasizes: 'the discourse of enterprise brooks no opposition between the mode of self-presentation required of consumers, managers and employees and the ethics of the personal self' (p. 64).

So far, then, it seems that there are plenty of reasons to suppose that recent changes in the public sector – specifically the ascendancy of a new managerialism – have led to changes in the personal identities of both professionals and managers, and perhaps especially to the identity of professional managers. New managerialist discourses have made up new ways for people to be at work. And these identities are being adopted by managers and professionals alike, partly in strategic career choices in a new climate and also, perhaps less 'consciously', as they are swept along by the tide of change.

The analyses by Miller and du Gay offer a far clearer elaboration of the links between managerial discourse and individual identity than has traditionally been the case in the literature on work and identity. Specifically, a breakdown has been offered of the processes through which identity is conferred. None the less, the emphasis in these accounts remains close to an initial assumption embedded in the more traditional and structural accounts, namely that organizations bend individual identities to their own imperatives (although both Miller and du Gay offer caveats on this point). The crucial difference between these newer accounts and more traditional versions is that organizationally imposed identities are no longer contrasted to an underlying 'true self'. Rather, identities are understood to be relational and conditional. That is to say, individual identities are not fixed in a transcendental human subject; nor are they fixed by key stages in childhood or even adult psychological development. Identities are continually in the process of being constructed, continually subject to change as the relations, practices and discourses which surround individuals change. Thus both Miller and du Gay are concerned with the discursive constitution of identity or, to use Hacking's (1986) phrase, with the ways in which people are 'made up'.

However, certain questions are still left begging. In particular, while identity may be reconceptualized as dynamic, there is still the tendency towards determinism, whereby 'work makes people'. There is little discussion of *agency* in these explanations of the construction of work identity in these newly imagined public sector organizations. And once agency is brought back into the picture, a multitude of new questions emerge. For example, have *all* public sector employees adapted in the ways described above? Have some resisted, or modified these changes? If so, how, and why? Restructuring may mean that new discourses present themselves, which in turn offer new possibilities for selfhood, but what factors determine the extent of the firmness of the embrace of managerialism, or enterprise, or calculation? And how consistent or coherent is this embrace?

New identities? Experiences of change

This section addresses the questions raised above, by focusing on empirical studies which offer insights into employees' responses to managerialism, whether as managers/professionals themselves, or as 'the managed'.

Teachers in the new managerialist climate

We begin by looking at this question in relation to professionals working in education, where increases in management responsibility across the hierarchy have been particularly sharp. As a result, the understanding of what a senior educational manager is has changed from an emphasis on superior professional skills to an emphasis on managerial acumen (Leonard 1998: 79).

It is, of course, head teachers who have had to take greatest personal responsibility for the new tasks and for the new philosophy. (See Menter and Muschamp, Chapter 5.) However, this role is not always adopted without conflict or regret. Head teachers in Levačić's (1995) study articulate mixed feelings:

> I am becoming more and more some sort of line manager, much more than a headteacher. I do very little teaching. I still feel guilty

about my lack of contact with the children. I am sure that parents would prefer a head who was seen more in the classroom.

(Horsefield head teacher, Levačić 1995: 118)

Heads are now much more line managers and I am not sure all heads are happy about this. Most headteachers are there because they are good teachers and show good practice in the classroom, and like interacting with and teaching children . . . Now that has been almost wiped away overnight . . . and there is a feeling of guilt that we should be doing more in the classroom.

(Pentland head teacher, p. 118)

Clearly, shifts are occurring in the ways that these head teachers see themselves at work, and the result is an uneasy mixture of old and new identities within individuals. The continued strength of an 'old' professional identity is reflected in the feelings of guilt which respondents cite at their loss of the role of 'teacher'. Furthermore, what also becomes clear from the empirical studies is that alongside the changes, there are differences which appear *between* individuals. While there are some people who are 'switched on' by the changes and identify with them, there are others who withdraw and retreat into areas of their work where they feel the 'new' culture doesn't touch them. This is very evident in Levačić's study of how head teachers have adapted to the introduction of local management of schools (LMS). 'Teacher A' comments that 'the head is enjoying LMS thoroughly. He works very hard. He gives the staff positive messages about it. The headteacher is the main motivator of staff' (Levačić 1995: 119). Meanwhile a different head teacher 'refuses' to play the new managerialist game:

I feel it is important to be more in touch with the children and so do minimal work on LMS. I want to be more accessible to parents so they can see me as someone closely involved with the children, rather than being locked away in an office and thus set apart.

(Fishlake head teacher, Levačić 1995: 119)

These contrasting responses were also found in Leonard's study of lecturers' responses to changes in further education. On the one hand a lecturer reported the endorsement of recent changes by many of her colleagues:

A masculine philosophy has come in culturally since Thatcher – in the last decade there is a machismo culture which has influenced everybody – personalities are falling in to this culture – but this culture was imbibed totally uncritically – a part of them that really liked that.

(Jenny, college section head, Leonard 1998: 79)

Another lecturer, however, reported strong personal feelings of hostility towards the newly privileged values and identities:

If I think about it, [I feel] upset and angry – and obviously you tend to think then of the things that are important, and concentrate on those: that is, the things over which I have control, the things I do in the classroom. I have consciously dropped out of the career game, as I didn't think I could change anything, and the more you progress, the more you get away from the things I happen to think are important: contact with students, the way to put things across to them, someone to talk to them, and look at their side of things. There's not a lot of opportunity to take that into management.

(Gwen, head of subject, Leonard 1998: 81)

Clearly, people respond differently to change. As Hargreaves (1994) explains, although changes may be very significant, people can adopt, adapt, resist or circumvent them as they arise (see Halford and Savage, forthcoming). While the theoretical analyses offered by writers such as Miller and du Gay emphasize the larger picture of change, they do so without bringing in the individual negotiations arising from a dialectical interplay of people's own identities – with their different intentions and resources – with the structurally determined conditions that confront them (Woods 1981). Woods's own research exemplifies this by concentrating on an earlier period of change in public sector education: comprehensivization. Looking at the stories of two teachers with very similar views about teaching, he found their responses to a period of rapid change to be very different. He accounts for this in the differences that could be found in their types of commitment and, more particularly for our purposes, their conceptions of identity. Whereas one teacher (Dick) was concerned to claim a particularly radical personal identity, another (Tom), though equally progressive in his educational philosophy, was quieter and detached. Whereas Dick tried to resist the ways in which the change was being managed, trying to confront and revolutionize the power structure, Tom worked to gain power within the system, and to influence those in the upper hierarchy. As Woods explains, '[i]f decisions were made that he did not like, he would not seek ways of overturning them but of adapting them' (Woods 1981: 298). Dick, by contrast, just 'wasn't going to bloody do it' (p. 298).

Woods's research demonstrates that some people see innovations and reforms as representing a threat to their sense of identity, and so will resist or adapt in order to try and maintain their old sense of self. This finding is echoed in Pollard's (1982) study of primary teachers. He found that although primary teachers do work under common structural constraints, they perceive them differently and react to them individually, making personal meanings (shaped by their personalities, biographies, and work contexts) out of similar situations and reacting to them in ways which have meaning for them. Nias also reveals 'significant divisions between individuals, within staffrooms, or within the profession at large' (Nias 1989: 30). For example, some teachers identify themselves as 'professionals' which means that first and foremost, their duty and concern is to their 'clients', for whom they strive to reach 'high professional standards' through 'good teaching'. By contrast, for some people the work identity is one they refuse to take on at all. For example, many of Nias's respondents did not 'see themselves' as teachers. For these people, any change at work is unlikely to affect their identity, as work is not part of the identity puzzle anyway. Still others identify themselves primarily as 'caring'. For them, teaching is very 'inclusive' (Argyris 1964 quoted in Nias 1989): that is, it absorbs much of their time and energy, and makes use of many of their talents and skills. These are teachers who, consciously or unconsciously, reduce the boundaries between their occupational and other lives (Nias 1989). Nias explains that these people tend to see teaching as a means of self-actualizing (Nias 1989: 17). By the same token, they were ready to leave teaching when they felt they were no longer being personally extended or that they had no time and energy to 'be themselves' outside the classroom, or that their uniqueness was under threat. Nias argues that the constraints in the 1988 Education Act may have had 'a damaging effect upon the commitment and self-expenditure of teachers such as these' (Nias 1989: 38), such as on the teacher in her study who complains:

> Before I started I used to think that I could set my own standards as a teacher . . . now I'm becoming a 'professional teacher'. I'm becoming compromised, falling back on what I know works, not on what is really me . . . I'll probably give up.
>
> (Nias 1989: 38)

The interesting thing about this last teacher's account is the way in which she is conscious of a division between one identity (what she calls her 'real self') and her professional identity. For her, the change to become a 'professional teacher' means adding another identity to the construction of her self; one which she does not really like, but which she can none the less perform. This sense of a 'splitting' in the sense of self is echoed above, in the accounts of those head teachers who acknowledged that they felt 'guilt': they were doing one thing (being managerial), but part of themselves felt they would also like to be doing another (classroom teaching).

These examples provide an important extension to the theoretical discussion of how identities are transformed through changing discourses, by suggesting that there may be points of fracture *within* people's identity, to the extent that identit*ies* may be a better term. Rather than acquiring a 'new identity' from the changing discursive context of work, it may be that another fraction is added to an already complex collection of identities. Thus not only do differences exist between individuals working in a context of change, but differences may also exist within individual identities themselves.

Such an internal jostling is well reflected in this head teacher's account:

Initially, I was philosophically opposed to local management, as I saw my role as an uncomplicated pressure for delivering an education service, and I had always seen it as other people's tasks to tell me how much money was available and how much of the service I wanted to provide I could or could not provide. I hoped I could be persuasive enough to wring resources out of the Authority to do the job. Part of me still feels this is a more honest way of proceeding but one mellows with the practicalities of life and we are now using the new system to our best advantage.

(Levačić 1995: 112)

Similarly, to recall the account by Jenny (above) of FE college managers' responses to the new managerialist policies, she explains that there was 'a part of themselves that really liked that . . . "thank goodness we can get back to this"' (Leonard 1998: 79).

For some people, the maintenance of these differences within themselves is a particularly conscious activity. Rather than adopting a new identity 'wholesale', they learn how to manage the work identity and keep it separate from their own lives (Nias 1989). Elliott (1976) also found that some teachers could teach with interest and conviction, but retain a sense of their other lives: 'I've learnt when to stop, when to have my own life'; 'My other interests enrich me: I'm not 100 per cent teacher'. Even 'those who made a positive choice to "become" teachers sometimes experienced periods of self-doubt or disillusion' (Nias 1989: 50). At such times, it was their out-of-school identities – as spouse, partner, parent or son/daughter – which became more important.

Managers in the new managerialist climate

These observations based specifically on education are endorsed by two broader studies of management and identity. Scase and Goffee (1989) found that although *in principle* managers are supportive of the enterprise ideal which has accompanied the recent restructuring exercises in both the public and private sectors, the expectation that they will become entrepreneurial jars with earlier training and experience and makes them anxious that suddenly everything rests on personality, rather than technical skill. Scase and Goffee (1989) conclude that the shift to the entrepreneurial manager is unlikely to take hold because of resistance from managers, who doubt their ability to manage through face-to-face negotiation and to exercise more personal forms of leadership. They are 'reluctant to shift from bureaucratic organizational modes of control because the introduction of flexible procedures would require them to be more immersed "psychologically" in their jobs' (p. 75). There is also resistance on the grounds of commitments to their life outside work: 'it increasingly appears that there are attempts to resist the potentially all-embracing "identity-conferring" attributes that corporate responsibilities often impose' (p. 138). To the contrary, Scase and Goffee offer evidence which suggests that managers 'maintain a cognitive distance between work role and self-identity' (p. 33), just performing adequately, abdicating 'any attempts to make significant creative, psychological or emotional contributions to their jobs' (p. 33). '[I]n the past, managers were more emotionally committed to their jobs and, as such, retirement was seen as a form of "premature death" . . . In the 1980s however, more seemed prepared for such lifestyles because they have consciously reduced their psychological dependence on work' (p. 100).

In fact, Scase and Goffee conclude that the impact of organizational restructuring as described above, combined with changing gender roles and increased middle class affluence (more leisure time, the consumer culture) means that managers personal identities 'are no longer solely derived from their jobs but, instead, are also shaped by a variety of non-work factors' (p. 180).

This is a conclusion which echoes Leinberger and Tucker's (1991) sequel to Whyte's (1956) study of *The Organization Man*. Whyte's study revealed how employees of large bureaucratic organizations derived their personal identity and sense of personal worth from those organizations. Not only were they totally bound up in the organization, but so were their wives and children: all were defined by the rank and business of the husband/father. Leinberger and Tucker interviewed the children of these organization men, and found a new breed of organizational employees, who orient themselves to their lives and work in ways which diverge sharply from their parents (Hargreaves 1994). Growing up in the post-war affluence of the 1950s, these children were released from the goals of competitive individualism, material struggle and the search for stability and security. Instead, the 1950s and the 1960s emphasized the goals of self-actualization, self-development and self-expression. However, on entering organizations as employees, this new generation of workers found work to be either indifferent or hostile to such self-oriented personal goals:

> Conventional bureaucratic organization suppressed or subordinated the self to the organization's needs, and were clearly antithetical to any pursuit of self-actualization and self-expression. Worse still, the radical restructurings brought about by the economic recession in the 1970s and 1980s, in the form of company closures, strategic break-up, compulsory redundancies and other bullish tactics of ever more separate administrations, ran directly counter to the fashionable rhetorics of individual empowerment, personal growth and corporate collaboration that characterized the new organizational 'glitterspeak'.
>
> (Hargreaves 1994: 65)

The members of the new generation responded to this 'organizational dismissal or denial of the self' in a number of ways. Some retreated from organizational life, some tried to reform it, some set up their own organizations. However, as Hargreaves explains in his analysis of the study, most interesting of all were those who exploited organizational structures for their own gain and satisfaction. They were constantly on the move, looking to work with people or on projects they liked, with no overall sense of loyalty or commitment to the company which employed them. *None* were 'organization men' (or women) in the conventional sense: 'for them, the traditional bond between the individual and the organization had been irreparably broken' (Hargreaves 1994: 66).

These empirical studies of the intersections of self and work in changing organizational contexts offer us some rich insights into our question on the extent of the impact of work on personal identity. For although as we have shown above, there is some strong theoretical and empirical evidence to suggest that changes in the public sector *have* had a substantial effect on identity (through changes in dominant discourses as well as alterations in the content of work roles), other evidence exists to suggest that these changes are experienced by individuals in ways which are somewhat 'patchy'. Not only do significant differences exist *between* people in the extent to which they take up these changes to their identity, but also differences exist *within* people, so that although they might perform in new ways at work, other parts of their identity, performed in other moments of time and space, may remain unaffected.

These findings enable us to make some important reflections on the ways in which work and identity are commonly understood. For it appears that neither the structural model (work determines identity) or the agentic model (identity determines how you work) which have dominated the sociology of work and organizations is wholly sufficient to explain the shifting, transitional and interactive picture of identity, or identities, which is appearing. Indeed, these empirical studies appear to raise some important questions about 'identity' per se. These concern, first, the question of *competing discourses* in the construction of identity (for example, in the case of teachers, why do some embrace new managerialism with alacrity, while others hold on to the model of the 'professional' or 'caring' teacher?); second, the *instability of identity* over time and space; and third, the place of *agency* in the construction of identity. In the final section of this chapter, we draw on some of the contemporary work on identity which is appearing in social and cultural theory which addresses these themes in order to explore some new ways of thinking about the relationships between identity and work.

Explorations of identity

Multiple/competing discourses?

Our first exploration concerns the relationship between the new managerialist discourse and other discourses which are also implicated in the construction of human subjectivity. How powerful is this discourse, and where does it sit in relation to all the other discourses which compete for a place in our construction of our selves? For du Gay (1996a), this is not an issue since he argues that 'enterprise' has assumed a near-hegemonic position in the construction of individual identities. That this is the case in the public sector just as much as elsewhere attests to the pervasiveness of the discourse. Furthermore, he claims, 'enterprise' has come to refer to far more than a particular form of managerialism. Rather, the enterprising self comes to dominate not just work life, but the totality of individuals' lives. Boundaries between work and home are broken down as the discourse of enterprise entails becoming a *better self*. The enterprising self is not simply '. . . just one among a plurality of ethical personalities' (du Gay 1996a: 181); rather, it assumes 'an ontological priority' (p. 181). Following Gordon's (1987) argument that 'the discourse of enterprise makes up the individual as a particular sort of person – as an "entrepreneur of the self"' (cited in du Gay 1986c: 11), du Gay claims that entrepreneurial discourse blurs distinctions, making entrepreneurial forms of conduct the most appropriate everywhere: 'every individual life is, in effect, structured as an enterprise of the self which each person must take responsibility for managing to their own best advantage' (du Gay 1996c: 14).

However, from our initial exploration of the empirical literature, it would appear that the discourse of enterprise remains simply one discourse among many – both within and outside work organizations – through which human identities are constituted. Although it is quite clear that the new managerialist discourse is flourishing right across the public sector, it has not totally displaced other frameworks of understanding about public sector work and organization. For example, teachers juggle new managerialism with the more traditional discourses of professionalism. Some prioritized one of these discourses, some acknowledged that they had shifted over time, while others resisted or adapted pressures to change themselves and the ways they work. Further, if we follow the argument which says that enterprise overrides everything, crossing all spheres and relationships, everything – being a lover, parent or golf player – becomes part of the all-consuming project of the self. While some might argue that this has indeed become the case (citing perhaps the plethora of 'self-help' books now available), once again, the empirical evidence confounds this position. Clearly, people perform a range of identities, in and out of work, reinforcing doubt that 'enterprise' forms such an ontological monolith. Rather, the coherence offered by 'enterprise' seems to crumble in the face of multiple and competing discourses.

In *Questions of Cultural Identity* Hall (1996: 4) suggests that: 'identities are never unified . . . never singular but multiply constructed across different, often intersecting and antagonistic discourses, practices and positions'.

Perhaps this is a useful way to think about the relationships between changes in the discourses which infuse work cultures and the construction of the self. Any new discourse – be it enterprise, managerialism or calculation – is not all-consuming, all-transformative: it merely *adds to* the complex, and often contradictory multiplicity of discourses to which all of us are subject. We are not simply pointing here to role-conflicts faced by individuals with complex commitments. The notion of role-conflict suggests that a core identity is faced with managing (or not managing) the different demands placed on that individual. Rather, we are suggesting that human identities are constructed from a range of subject positions; and that each of us is subject to diverse and sometimes competing discourses which constitute our identity in multiple and fractured ways. In short, we are not 'a coherent relational system. Demands co-exist . . . which are diverse, conflicting, and disorderly' (Laplanche and Pontalis 1985, quoted in Hall 1996: 3). New managerialist discourse can therefore only be one component in the construction of individual identities.

Instability over time and space

We have argued above for a discursive conceptualization of identity which emphasizes the operation of multiple and (sometimes) competing discourses. It is important to point out that the 'result' is not a stable identity – albeit multiple and complex – which remains fixed across time and space. Rather, individual identities shift over time and space – a suggestion given some initial support by our exploration of the empirical literature. The question of *scale* is important here. In delineating the differences between understandings of identity in modern and postmodern times, Bauman (1996) dismisses the once popular notion that individual identities form cumulatively over an individual's lifetime. Instead, he suggests, '[t]ime is no longer a river, but a collection of pools and ponds' (p. 25). The imagery used suggests temporary stagnations over a lifetime, a spreading out into relatively stable identities for periods of time but inevitable movement on to new and only tenuously connected identities. Thus Bauman implies the replacement of one identity with another over the life course. But could it be that individuals move backwards and sideways, as well as forward, between identities? And could it be that these shifts take place within days or even hours, rather than across years or lifetimes?

In addition to temporal mobility, identities may be spatially mobile. That is to say, identity may be fragmented across space. For instance, an individual's sense of self may shift between organizational space and other spaces, or even between spaces within organizations. This is well illustrated in Nippert-Eng's (1996) study of the 'boundaries' which exist between home and work. While some people are happy for the two spaces to be highly 'integrated', so that who they are at work is almost indistinguishable from who they are at home, others attempt to keep the two highly distinct: conceiving them, and themselves within them, as two completely separate and segmented spaces:

> the self becomes separated, parcelled out so that certain aspects of identity are emphasised in one realm, others in its opposite. The ways we spatially and temporally divide up objects, people and activities reflect and promote the mental boundaries we place around these certain ways of being, of thinking, and of acting.
>
> (Nippert-Eng 1996: 34)

Nippert-Eng suggests that we all create and maintain more or less distinct 'territories of the self' (1996: 28), categorizing aspects of our selves into discrete geographical places and times of the day, week or year. For many people, however, the two identities – those of inside and outside work – are not totally distinct. Rather, there is a two-way flow between work and non-work, and parts of each identities are transported into the other sector. Work may be done at home in bed, and sexual liaisons may take place in the workplace. Pringle's (1989) work on secretaries also demonstrated how people may perform their 'domestic' identities at work, acting as mother or wife to their bosses. Clearly, identities are both multiple and transportable. As Nippert-Eng argues, people carve out their identities in different places and at different times, with decision making about where to place the boundaries and with whom, and how to enact and maintain these, being a more-or-less continual process.

The recognition that identity is highly fluid, and changeable across time and space, presents a challenge to the idea that new managerialist discourses have a transformative effect on identity. Individuals might well feel 'enterprising' on occasion, whether at work or even at home, in bed, with the kids or on the golf course, but then not so at other moments. In other words, differences exist as to where and when a new 'self' may be constructed; at certain times, in certain places and with certain people a 'managerialist' self may be performed, while at others it might be hotly rejected. Clearly, too, differences exist between people as to the extent of the impact of new managerialist discourses on their identities. Some people may 'buy in' with pleasure, whereas others refuse to change in any way.

Agency

These speculations lead us to return to one of the central concerns of this chapter, which is to look at the ontological nature of the relationship between changing work discourses and identity. Do we really take on the new identity associated with new managerialism, enterprise or accountancy? Are these identities simply etched onto individual psyches through a top-down discursive imposition, or 'labelling from above' (Hacking 1986)? From our empirical review, it seems not. Rather, individuals appear to take a more agentic role in evaluating the new managerialism, and placing themselves in relation to it.

In some cases it seems that managers make an active decision to use the new managerialist rhetoric for their own ends. Cochrane's (1993) analysis of recent changes in local government suggests that '[m]any key professionals are seeking legitimacy . . . from their ability to fit in with the latest management language' (p. 106) which offers them a new credibility and status: 'Senior managers in local government are now able to claim a powerful role with a higher status than that of the welfare professionals they have had to manage' (p. 120).

Similarly, also commenting on local government, Stoker (1990: 251) concluded that: 'Change occurs because of the self-interested judgements of individuals or groups about what is/is not working and what is/is not beneficial to them and their supporters.'

However, this active adoption of new managerialist positions should not lead us to assume that managers' identities are becoming coterminous with managerialist discourse. Rather, it is possible that some managers deliberately portray managerialist identities while maintaining a quite different sense of self. Goffman (1969) termed this practice of taking on and using social scripts 'impression management'. Describing the individual performances involved, Goffman suggested that personal commitment to the impression being enacted could range from those who believed totally in what they were trying to do, to those who didn't believe in it at all (see also Crang 1994 on performance work in restaurant work, and Nias 1989 on primary teachers). As Cohen (1994) argues, people may take on 'socially scripted personhood' but that is not necessarily to say that their sense of self undergoes an identical transformation. Or, to complicate matters further, perhaps sometimes people believe their own performances, and sometimes they don't (perhaps in relation to time and space, as we discussed above). Furthermore, as we saw in the previous section, it is possible that people will choose to reject the identity associated with new managerialism altogether, resisting and continuing to display alternative performances. Hence the relationship between new managerialist discourse and individual identity may be one of ambivalence, or even resistances, as well as a more straightforward process of adoption. Individuals may retain continued commitment to professionalism or to non-market notions of public service; or they may be highly sceptical of the relevance of private sector managerial paradigms for public sector management (Newman and Clarke 1994).

Conclusions

It would appear from our exploration of the impact of new managerialist discourses on the identities of managers and professionals working in the public sector, that although the influence of these discourses is undeniable, processes appear to exist which seem to 'interrupt, prevent or disturb the smooth insertion of individuals into the subject positions constructed by those discourses' (Hall 1996: 11). As yet, we do not have sufficient evidence to enable us to let go of either side of the structure–agency dichotomy. However, what has become clearer from our study is that each of these concepts has to be understood as complex – each has been split and fractured by a multiplicity of differences. On the one hand, discourses compete and jostle with each other. As Miller (1992) points out, despite its ascendancy in recent years, accountancy is not the only discourse, and battles will take place as 'rival expertises or other groups seek to reaffirm, redefine, extend or simply protect their own domains' (p. 80). Thus the discursive construction of self can never be simply read off from one particular discourse, since alternative discourses always exist (compare du Gay's superior 'enterprise' discourse).

On the other hand, people situate themselves in different relationships to the variety of discourses. As we have seen from our study of the empirical literature, particular individuals have their own histories which will mediate the impact of any single discourse on the construction of the self. Indeed, that this is the case is recognized by both du Gay and Miller: 'although enterprise prefers a *tabula rasa* upon which to write its compositions, it actually seeks to produce its effects under circumstances not of its own choosing' (du Gay 1996a: 150).

More broadly, Miller argues that government generally, and economic calculation as one form of government, are 'congenitally failing' operations (1992: 74, 79): 'the technologies of accountancy often intersect poorly with the specifics of the "real". The conditions that would make them work "perfectly" are frequently absent, unplanned outcomes emerge, and new situations make existing technologies obsolete' (p. 79).

Employees in the public sector come to work with their own personal agenda, such that the degree to which their identity is changed by new discourses in the workplace is highly variable. Certainly restructuring might mean the presentation of alternative discourses, offering new possibilities for self-hood. However, we cannot assume that this is in any way an automatic or linear process; or that individuals respond in ways which are consistent or coherent. The interesting point to look for, as the process of restructur*ing* consolidates into the restructur*ed*, is the extent to which the intersections between discourse and identity bring about mutations in the 'new managerialist' public sector organizations themselves.

8 | Assessment and conclusions

Mark Exworthy and Susan Halford

Introduction: taking an overview

The past 20 years have seen profound changes within the UK public sector. The chapters in this book have shown that changes to professional work, to managerial work, and a shifting relationship between the two, have been central to this transformation. The preceding chapters have contributed to our knowledge and understanding of the nature and extent of this transformation by focusing on three areas of the public sector: education, medicine and social work. Taken together, these chapters offer a great deal of evidence and argument with which to document, assess and interpret contemporary change in each sector specifically and in the public sector more generally.

In Chapter 1 we suggested that there were good reasons for supposing that the outcomes of professional–managerial relations in the public sector would be characterized by contingency and chaos. Despite popular and academic notions of professional–managerial antipathy and conflict, we argued that, in practice, professional–managerial relations were likely also to be characterized by relations of compromise and collaboration. Certainly, the chapters in this collection offer examples of all three outcomes. In Chapter 2 Rob Flynn argued that essential differences between management and professions continue to persist and, indeed, that during the recent squeeze on public expenditure, conflict is likely to be further exacerbated by arguments over resource allocation. In Chapter 3, Chris Jones also found evidence of continued conflict, this time between social work professionals and the new managerialism which he links to the New Right in British politics. In the battle between the two, Jones concludes that social work as a profession is losing out, as something approaching a managerial takeover occurs. Taking a rather different focus, Chapters 5 and 7 also offered evidence of conflict. Ian Menter and Yolande Muschamp documented teachers' private hostility to managerially imposed changes in education, particularly the new classroom assessment procedures and indicators of staff performance. Menter and Muschamp conclude that while teachers might present a public face which supports the recent changes in education, in private they feel demoralized and alienated. Similarly, Susan Halford and Pauline Leonard show that teachers, and even general managers from a range of sectors, often feel a great deal of personal hostility to the values and practices associated with managerialism.

But as well as this evidence of conflict, we have also been offered plenty of examples where there has been compromise and collaboration between professionals and managers. Despite his analysis of the fundamental differences between professionalism and managerialism in social work, in Chapter 3 Jones acknowledges that professional social workers are in fact increasingly adopting managerial roles. In Chapter 4 Stephen Harrison also provides evidence that a merging of professional and managerial roles is taking place, this time in medicine. In this instance there is apparently no explicit evidence of conflict. Doctors are taking on managerial responsibilities and, *at the same time*, maintaining both clinical autonomy and professional identity. Head teachers too are taking on major managerial responsibilities (see Chapter 5: 69–75) for the most part with relish and aplomb. Indeed, reviewing evidence from across medicine, nursing, education and social work, Gordon Causer and Mark Exworthy conclude that compromise and collaboration between managerial and professional roles has now become so commonplace that exclusionary categories of 'manager' and 'professional' are no longer adequate to describe the range of accommodations which are being made between the two.

In Chapter 1 we suggested that the outcome of professional–managerial relations in particular instances would, in part, be influenced by the structural features of individual sectors within the welfare state; by the nature of managerialism (including the degree of marketization) within that sector; and by the level of professionalization attained by different professional groups. Certainly each of these factors has been shown to be important. In medicine, for instance, where professional privilege is guaranteed by state-backed controls on the right to practise, it seems that doctors have been particularly 'successful' in protecting their territory and authority. By contrast, in social work, where professionalism has never achieved the same degree of autonomy or status, the managerialist challenge appears to have eroded professional privilege more rapidly and more thoroughly. Interestingly, however, this outcome has emerged despite the fact that the degree of marketization in the health care sector (in which medicine operates) has, to date, been far greater than is the case in social work. This demonstrates that the interplay between the three factors described above is, in practice, quite difficult to predict.

More than this, however, these structural or contextual factors alone do not adequately account for the range of outcomes in professional–managerial relations documented in the preceding chapters. Indeed, our chapters suggest different outcomes within the *same* sector and where apparently similar levels of professionalization and managerialism co-exist. Compare, for example, Jones's analysis of the inherent antagonism between 'managerialism' and 'professionalism' in social work with the material on managerial-professional social workers presented in Causer and Exworthy's chapter. Furthermore, taken together, our chapters contain some fundamental contradictions. For example, if essential differences between professions and management persist, as Flynn argues in Chapter 2, how can we understand the growth of managerial professionals documented by Causer and Exworthy in Chapter 6?

Where do these 'contradictions' leave us? Are we left to conclude, quite simply, that contingency reigns? Does the evident chaos render us unable to make comparisons between professional–managerial relations in different sectors? Does it become impossible to take an overview of professional–managerial interactions in the contemporary public sector or to make any more general conclusions about professional–managerial relations? How can we make comparisons between our chapters, or the sectors more broadly, when the 'results' appear so chaotic? Consequently, what are the implications of answers to these questions for our theoretical understandings of professionals and managers?

In this chapter, we suggest two rather different ways forward. First, we suggest that the chaos may be rendered more orderly by recognizing that different authors/pieces of research (both here and in the literature more broadly) are actually focusing on quite different dimensions of the professional–managerial relation even if they *appear* to be looking at the same thing. Thus one of the reasons why comparisons and overarching conclusions are difficult (and, indeed, rarely undertaken) is because different studies are not, in fact, comparing like with like. We elaborate on this point in the next section, where we offer a simple framework to explain the different dimensions of analysis present within the literature. We do not claim that placing existing research within this framework will structure divergent research outcomes into a coherent pattern, or erase the diversity of outcomes documented by existing research on professional–managerial relations. More modestly, however, we do believe that our framework clarifies *some* of the causes of difference between previous pieces of research and, in doing so, helps to define an agenda for research in the future. Second, we suggest that, bearing this in mind, we can reassess the more abstract, theoretical arguments about professional–managerial relations presented in Chapter 1. In 'Making some conclusions' we use the evidence from our chapters to reconsider arguments about post-Fordism and post-bureaucratic control, also arguments about the nature of 'assets', and claims about the fragmentation of lateral solidarities within professions. We end this chapter with some more speculative conclusions about future directions in professional– managerial relations in the public sector, considering specifically the impact of the Labour government elected in May 1997.

Analysing professional–managerial relations

The evidence and ideas about professional–managerial relations presented in this book are, on the face of it, difficult to compare, or to take an overview of, for a number of reasons. Quite deliberately, we chose contributors who would draw on a range of social scientific disciplines including sociology, social policy, politics and management studies. This was intended to build a fuller picture of contemporary professional–managerial relations in the public sector than would be offered by any one discipline, and thereby to begin a dialogue about the value of different concepts, methods and analyses. Furthermore, by choosing to compare three different parts of the public sector, our book inevitably reflects the specific bodies of knowledge developed by the professionals and academics, or 'knowledge elite' (Freidson 1994) associated with each sector. Cross-cutting these points about disciplinary and sectoral diversity, our book includes contributions with quite different theoretical underpinnings. For example, compare the structuralist approach taken by Jones, with the more (neo)-Weberian account offered by Flynn and the poststructuralist influence evident in the chapter by Halford and Leonard.

In other words, the impression that professional–managerial relations are diverse and unpredictable is not surprising! It is not our role here to arbitrate between the different disciplines, sectoral knowledges, theories or methodologies, or to attempt to establish the validity of different accounts. However, at the same time, it *is* our role to attempt some reconciliation of the diverse impressions presented in this book. We want to be able to make some general conclusions about how professional–managerial relations are changing and to suggest ways forward for future research. In what follows we suggest that a first step towards achieving this is to recognize that existing research, presented in this book and elsewhere, tends to focus on quite different dimensions of the professional–managerial relation *but rarely acknowledges that this is so*, or the significance of this difference. While they may appear to be addressing the same issues, in fact different dimensions of the issue are being examined. By defining each of these different dimensions, and their relation to one another, we can provide a framework which encompasses each of our chapters and, indeed, research on professional–managerial relations more broadly. We can then begin to 'unpick' the key aspects of contemporary change in professional–managerial relations without privileging a particular discipline, theory or methodology. We hope that, as a result, we can clarify and facilitate comparative research.

An analytical framework

In seeking to ascertain the nature of change, it is possible to identify three different dimensions of professional–managerial relations upon which

existing research has focused. While some studies focus on abstract concepts and ideas about change, others address the collective role of professionals and management, while others still focus on the way in which
individual work tasks, roles and identities are changing. (See Ferlie *et al.*
1996: 168 for a related discussion about the analysis of the individual and
the collective.)

The 'abstract' dimension concerns the conceptual and ideological
aspects of the articulation between 'professionals' and 'managers' and/or
'professionalism' and 'managerialism'. Here we are concerned with
efforts to define what 'professionalism' is or what 'managerialism' is and,
often, to mark out at an abstract level what distinguishes one from the
other. Flynn's work in Chapter 2 is precisely in this territory, delineating
fundamental and irresolvable differences at the core of 'professionalism'
and 'managerialism'. This dimension might also encompass abstract
ideas about individual identity: ideas about how we should understand
'identity', whether as determined by structural relations in a rather fixed
way or discursively constructed and rather more fluid (see for example
Chapter 7). Similarly this dimension may also include different abstractions about 'the state' – whether this is seen as a mechanism of advancing
social class privilege (see for example Chapter 3) or as a more contested
site of diverse social relations. Drawing attention to this dimension of
analysis is clearly not to privilege any one set of abstractions, nor any
single theoretical position. Nor, therefore, is it to suggest a causality from
the abstract to the collective or individual. The 'three-dimensional'
framework should not be seen as hierarchical but relational – that is, each
dimension is interconnected with each other. One dimension thus does
not, by itself, precipitate change in another.

The second dimension is that of the 'collectivity'. This refers to the collective body of *professions* and *management(s)* and, as such, is concerned with
the institutional and organizational dimensions of these social groupings. It follows that issues of concern at this dimension would include the
internal stratification of professions and management, and the social capital underpinning the coherence and cohesiveness of both groups. While
all professions have been affected by the managerialization of the public
sector, the impact has been differentially felt, not least because some professions have been actively incorporated into the changes. For example,
general practitioners have been given the opportunity to become 'fundholders' and therefore have a degree of control over budgets. Not all GPs
have wished (or been able) to become a fundholder and, moreover, other
related professions (for example nursing) have not had this opportunity.
The situation is somewhat different in (for example) education, given its
unidisciplinary context. However, the stratification of the teaching profession has been increased with the devolution of (financial) responsibility to head teachers and departmental heads. Causer and Exworthy
(Chapter 6) conclude that, while the significance of managerial professionals is generally increasing, managerial competencies are becoming

more important for all professional groups. Harrison (Chapter 4) clearly points out that managerialization is incorporating professionals, with the consequence that the stratification of the medical profession is becoming more pronounced. The composition and maintenance of lateral solidarities is thus an important component of this collectivity dimension.

The third dimension concerns the 'individual'. The outcome(s) of professional–managerial interactions will vary between and even within individual professionals and managers. Many of the processes mentioned earlier will be played out at the individual level both *between* individual professionals and managers and even *within* individuals. As such, the 'individual' dimension of analysis will be concerned with, among others, changing identity (identities) as well as job titles, tasks and career paths and so on (Halford and Savage 1997). Halford and Leonard (Chapter 7) argue that individual identities may encompass both professional and managerial components and that the relation between the two may be unstable and fluctuating across both time and space. Likewise, Causer and Exworthy (Chapter 6) suggest that, within individuals, the role of the managerial professional is increasingly blurring the distinctions between individual professional and managerial roles. Menter and Muschamp (Chapter 5) also conclude that, while teachers might present a public face which supports the recent (managerial) changes in education, in private, they feel demoralized and alienated.

This delineation of these three dimensions of analysis helps to explain some of the confusion evident when comparing studies of professional–managerial relations. In short, different studies are not always comparing 'like with like'. Recognizing this, it becomes less meaningful to attempt a simple comparison between Flynn's arguments about inherent difference between 'professionalism' and 'managerialism' with Causer and Exworthy's evidence about managerial professionals. While recognition of the three dimensions of analysis does not do away with contradictions and paradoxes, they may become more easily understood and accommodated. Simply put, what you find will depend on where you look. However, in suggesting that professional–managerial relations are constituted along all three dimensions and that existing research tends to situate itself within one of these dimensions (or to combine a focus on two dimensions – see below), a number of further questions arise, concerning both the analytical and methodological implications of this framework.

Analytical questions

In this section, we examine the analytical and theoretical implications of the three-dimensional framework discussed above, assessing its contribution to our understanding of professional–managerial relations. In doing so, we appraise the status of the three dimensions employed and assess their interrelationships.

Status of the three dimensions
The framework is designed as a way of seeing and interpreting the articulation between professionals and managers, as individuals, as groups and in abstract terms. It is not specifically intended as an explanatory tool. The framework encourages a move away from a sole focus on the content and type of professional–managerial interaction (for example conflict, compromise and collaboration) towards more explicit consideration of the level of analysis: where are we looking as well as what are we looking at? Given the contingency identified earlier in this book, this shift seems appropriate. In many senses, the type of approach we take intimately affects the understanding we have of the nature and outcome of professional–managerial interaction. Identification of conflict, compromise and collaboration (as in Chapter 1) is a useful starting point in any analysis of this sort but it does not take overall understanding much further. Thus the dichotomous depiction of professionals and managers as necessarily in conflict with each other is not as straightforward as is often portrayed. We need, however, in order to extend the analysis further than the identification of alternative outcomes, to develop more sensitive analytical perspectives. However, if the framework will not necessarily be able to determine the outcomes of professional–managerial interactions, we can at least begin to identify the components of analysis that will be needed to offer a comprehensive understanding of professional–managerial relations. As such, the framework acts essentially as a heuristic device to aid our understanding rather than as a predictive tool. It is therefore not a representation of actual interactions but, rather, a distillation of multifarious empirical and theoretical evidence from the professional–managerial literature generally, and this book specifically.

In fact, the primary value of the dimensions, individually and collectively, lies primarily in their methodological contribution (see 'Methodological implications' below) because of the level of detail or focus that they offer. Given that the purpose of the framework is not necessarily to predict the outcome of interactions, it does, nevertheless, have some interpretive power: namely, its ability to explain why some conclusions might appear to conflict with those of other studies of, say, the same sector, profession and/or issue. This (re-)emphasizes that studies need to be clear about the dimension in which their research is based. Often, this is not sufficiently explained or stated; usually it is an implicit assumption of the text.

Interrelationship between dimensions
The *boundaries* between these three interlocking dimensions are not fixed. Certainly we see that degrees of overlap between dimensions might occur; this is illustrated in those studies which incorporate elements of more than one dimension. The contributors' chapters illustrate most of the components of this framework; most exemplify some degree of overlap between dimensions. Flynn's chapter (Chapter 2) deals essentially

with the abstract dimension; Harrison's (Chapter 4) with the collectivity dimension; and Menter and Muschamp's (Chapter 5) with the individual dimension. By contrast, Jones examines how the professionalism of social work has impacted upon the training of individual social workers, thereby combining the abstract and individual dimensions. Causer and Exworthy (Chapter 6) address the emergence of the managerial professional as an example of the fragmentation of lateral solidarities, as well as the identity and authority issues that emerge from such a role. Halford and Leonard (Chapter 7) take a different perspective by combining the abstract and individual dimensions, through a conceptual analysis of the meaning of multiple and fractured identities within individual professionals and managers.

The *relationship between each of the three dimensions* should be seen, for our purposes here, as relational rather than hierarchical. We have thus avoided the terms macro, meso and micro, or top-down and bottom-up; to do so would be to presume a hierarchical and sequential ordering of the 'levels' of analysis. For example, the collectivity dimension can be viewed independently or in conjunction with the other two. Likewise, a hierarchy would imply that the collectivity dimension would be 'located' 'between' the abstract and individual dimensions. We wanted to avoid that impression. The nature of the interrelationship between dimensions in the framework depends, to a great extent, upon the theoretical perspective taken. Different theoretical positions would derive different interpretations and outcomes from the framework. For example, a structuralist perspective would presume a hierarchical and causal relationship stemming from the abstract dimension to the other two. We would rather see the abstract as more than just a structural dimension, although the framework could incorporate such a perspective.

Taking these points about overlap and about the relation between the three dimensions together, our framework can therefore be represented graphically by means of a Venn diagram (see Figure 8.1).

Implicit in this diagram are the interconnections of each dimension; each is related to each of the other dimensions and can thus be used in analytical exercises jointly or separately with others. It shows not only the differences between the dimensions but also what connects them. Taken together, the three dimensions represent the cumulative body of work concerning professional–managerial relations. Any individual study might focus on one or more dimensions, whereas the corpus of knowledge is represented by all three dimensions.

Methodological implications

Because we have intended the framework to be an aid to understanding (rather than one which predicts the outcomes of professional–managerial interactions), it follows that its implications will be largely in terms of

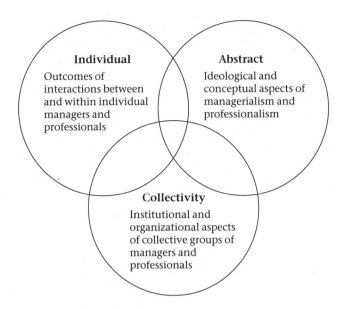

Figure 8.1   Three-dimensional analytical framework

methodological application. We foresee two prime instances in which these implications will have most effect: comparative analyses, and the (limited) power of conclusions that can be drawn. These applications thus qualify the framework.

We identified, at the start of this chapter, that inferring conclusions from such diversity was problematic unless there was a device which recognized different levels of analysis, sectors and theoretical standpoints. Although the framework is but one way in which this diversity can be accommodated, it demands that greater clarity is taken in specifying more explicitly which dimension (or dimensions) is (are) being adopted, the nature and understanding of that dimension, and its (their) inter-connections and articulation with other dimensions in the framework. Only by doing so can one be certain about the conclusions that can be inferred from such studies.

The second methodological application concerns the partiality of such conclusions in studies of the articulation between professionals and man-agers (or their respective collective bodies or ideologies). It follows from the previous argument about the need for clarity in comparative analyses that the explanatory power and conclusions that such studies can gener-ate is somewhat limited. In recognizing the three dimensions proposed in this framework, it would appear likely that most studies would focus on only one dimension, or possibly two. Few studies have been large or ambitious enough to employ all three. If the framework is accepted, then it is inevitable that the conclusions drawn from many studies will be par-tial. While this inference was also drawn in Chapter 1 concerning the contingency and chaos that professional–managerial relations were likely to produce, we have developed the argument further here. We can be more definitive as a result of recognizing the dimensions which each study incorporates.

It may, therefore, be likely to prove difficult to reach encompassing conclusions in such studies. However, the literature as a whole may be able to do so by, in effect, addressing all three dimensions. It should be to help us learn the lessons from other sectors and studies while, at the same time, recognizing the scope and limitations of each. This book is intended to act as a contribution to the overall 'professional–managerial' literature by being cumulative and intersectoral.

Making some conclusions

Explicit recognition of the different dimensions of analysis, as described above, makes sweeping general conclusions rather difficult about each of our three sectors (social work/teaching/medicine), the public sector more generally, or professional–managerial relations more generally still. Where abstract argument or collective groups might make one claim, there will always be counterexamples at the level of individual analysis. Of course this is a condition under which most – if not all – academic analysis operates. None the less, in the first section of this chapter we argued that an *explicit* recognition of the different dimensions of analysis represented in work on professional–managerial relations would help to clarify some of the competing outcomes and apparent contingency evident within our book and within the field more generally. Having said this, however, we do want to move forward and make some broader conclusions. In what follows, we reflect on the implications of this research evidence for theoretical debates about the nature and future of professional–managerial relations.

Research evidence and theoretical debates

In Chapter 1 we introduced three bodies of theoretical work and suggested that they might be particularly important in thinking about recent changes in professional–managerial relations. These concerned, first, questions of post-Fordism and the emergence of a new 'post-bureaucratic' form of organizational control; second, the notion of differential 'assets' as the key line of distinction between professionals and managers; and third, the suggestion that the major threat to the future of professions comes from within, through the erosion of lateral solidarities. The questions raised by these theories have resurfaced throughout the chapters in this book along the different dimensions of analysis identified above. We now return directly to these ideas in order to reassess them in the light of our chapters. In each case, while the focus begins with the abstract, conceptual dimension the debate can be extended by bringing in examples from the collective and individual dimensions of analysis.

Post-Fordism and post-bureaucratic control
In short, work within this paradigm suggests that an ongoing transformation in the global economy is taking place, and that this is reflected at the level of organization, particularly with the emergence of new forms of 'flexible' organization and new forms of organizational control. The latter depends not so much on centralization and formal discipline over staff but on more devolved and internalized disciplinary mechanisms among staff with much greater degrees of organizational freedom. Hoggett (1991) refers to this as 'regulated autonomy', precipitating a reassessment of our understandings in favour of 'paradox and contradiction rather than the either/or binary logic of the past' (Hoggett 1996: 24). Intimately linked to new managerialist discourses, the suggestion that organizations, and organizational control, are undergoing such a fundamental revolution clearly also has implications for the place and practice of professionals in welfare state bureaucracies (see the discussion in Chapter 1).

The material presented in this book has clear resonances with many of the themes associated with post-Fordism and post-bureaucratic control. Arising from processes of marketization and decentralization, the essential themes discussed here include fragmentation, fracturing, and new alliances between and within professionals and managers. Flynn (Chapter 2) examined the processes by which the abstract notions of professionalism and managerialism were being challenged. These processes were also explored through different dimensions, and using different theories, by Harrison (Chapter 4) and Jones. Both, however, foresee that the processes of change are precipitating a reordering of professions and management.

One of the key claims within post-Fordist debates is that the welfare state is undergoing a process of 'hollowing out', whereby functions and responsibilities are being centralized and devolved and sub-contracted, in such a way that there is 'little left in the middle' (Jessop 1994). This claim links more abstract arguments about post-Fordism to the collective and individual dimensions, as the hollowing out displaces powers between professionals–professions as well as between professionals–professions and managers–management. The displacement in relation to professionals and managers has primarily taken place downwards and outwards.

The displacement downwards is primarily linked to decentralization, an essential feature of post-Fordist organizations. Much of the decentralist policy in the UK public sector has been managerial in nature and has encroached upon domains and territory previously the province of professionals (Exworthy 1992). For example, the structure of nurse management has been largely eroded by the introduction of NHS general management at increasingly lower organizational levels. Thus the acceptance or resistance towards such displacement will be differentially felt by the relative power of professions and according to the type of decentralization (Hoggett 1991) – financial decentralization impacting more significantly upon professionals than, say, geographical decentralization. The former may, as Harrison implied, implicate professionals in resource and allocative decision making. The role of managerial professionals, as shown by Causer and Exworthy, has a bearing upon the decentralist impact. They can act as a buffer between rank-and-file professionals and the decentralizing management. However, this is often at some expense to their authority and identity.

The displacement outwards to agencies on a contractual basis is integral to the marketization of sectors (Pinch 1997). The resulting organizational competition pits manager against manager and professional against professional. The organization becomes the principal axis rather than the professional–managerial one. As such, it is a 'zero sum' game in which 'gains' are made at the expense of 'losses' elsewhere. Menter and Muschamp and Jones demonstrated how the displacement of these powers is not accepted unconditionally and is invariably contested. One impact, Halford and Leonard showed, was the fracturing of individual identities. Another impact concerned the process described by Causer and Exworthy: the role of managerial professionals. Hoggett (1991, 1994) sees this development of this development of this role as indicative of post-bureaucratic control. Here, marketization and 'operational disaggregation' increasingly implicate managerial professionals in the running of that organization. Through these structural processes, the nature of control/discretion among individual professionals and managers is redefined.

However, some dispute the implications of post-Fordism upon the public sector especially in relation to professional work. Mohan (1995) claims that the work of doctors, for example, was never under managerial control in the Fordist sense and, indeed, the discretion associated with professional work militated against Fordist principles – a reason, some suggest, for placing them under (some form) of state control in the first place. Furthermore, some claim the equivocal nature of much of the evidence about post-Fordism undermines the analysis in connection with professional–managerial relations. For example, while Hoggett (1991) clearly states that professional–managerial 'conflicts are not so much being extended, as transcended', he does add that post-Fordism is 'agnostic' about the future. Hence, the post-Fordist interpretation of the outcomes of professional–managerial interactions remains somewhat uncertain. Similarly, Mohan (1995) argues that the dichotomy between Fordism and post-Fordism has tended to exaggerate the significance of change since 1979.

Nevertheless, this brief discussion of post-Fordism and post-bureaucratic control has highlighted the connections between the redefinition and recomposition of the public sector, the welfare state and their constituent professions and managements. It has also aided our understanding of the possible consequences for individual professionals and managers.

Professional and managerial assets
A key distinction between professionals and managers has been made in terms of the particular assets possessed by each group (see the discussion of Savage *et al.* in Chapter 1 for further analysis). To recap, it has been argued that professionals depend on 'cultural' assets, acquired through education and characterized by personal expertise in a given body of practice, while managers depend on 'organizational' assets, acquired through the experience of working in particular contexts and characterized by knowledge of organizationally specific rules, practices and politics. However, the material presented in this book suggests that professional and managerial work, and the assets held by professionals and managers, may no longer be so distinct. Looking at the chapters in this book, Menter and Muschamp as well as Jones demonstrate that the competencies required by individual professionals have shifted quite significantly in recent years. Head teachers are now, more or less, managing directors; social workers are now 'care managers'. Similarly, Causer and Exworthy document how professionals, individually and collectively, have incorporated and have been incorporating managerial skills into their roles with the consequence, they argue, that distinctions between the two groups are increasingly blurred. Arguably, however, it is not simply that professionals are acquiring assets traditionally associated with managers, but also that the assets associated with managers are changing too.

In fact, it seems that the new managerialism is actually *loosening* the ties between management and organizational assets. At the heart of the new managerial paradigm lies a faith in *generic* management skills, applicable across a *range* of public and private sector organizations. Commitment to this has been widely illustrated over recent years (Newman and Clarke 1994). For example, the 1983 NHS Management Inquiry (known as the Griffiths Report) proposed *generic* managers, regardless of discipline, to overcome the lack of 'a clearly defined *general* management function' (para. 4, emphasis added). This new managerialism stresses the importance of *individual* qualities and competencies over individuals' knowledge of (or ability to apply) specific bureaucratic procedures. The emphasis is on empowering others further down the organizational hierarchy rather than knowing exactly how particular tasks are or should be done. Managerial authority is thus still linked to hierarchical position, but it is far less embedded in the details of bureaucratic life than has traditionally been the case. Managerial assets may well still be distinct from the cultural assets typically associated with professionals, but it may no longer be accurate to regard these as 'organizational' assets. Indeed, as managers are becoming increasingly credentialled (witness the rise of management degrees at both undergraduate and postgraduate level) and able to transfer these credentials across organizations, it may be increasingly accurate to regard 'managerial' assets as another form of 'cultural' asset, and not as 'organizational' assets at all.

Looking at the other side of the coin, it is clear from the chapters in this book that organizational assets – or more accurately in the present context, *managerial* assets – are becoming far *more* important for professional staff. An important distinction has been acknowledged here between the older professions (principally law and medicine) – with established (and legally protected) independence – and the newer 'mediative professions' (such as social work), which only emerged on a large scale in the context of expanding public bureaucracies (Savage *et al.* 1992; Freidson 1994). *Organizational* assets have always had more significance for these latter professions but, more recently, *managerial* assets have become far more significant for *all* professional staff. For the aspiring professional it is no longer sufficient to possess professional cultural assets alone, though these still bear authority and status. Professionals may also need to acquire and demonstrate managerial assets in addition if, as individuals, they wish to progress in their careers or if, as a group, they want to retain their privileges. Indeed, as Savage *et al.* (1992) argue, 'career' is becoming a far more useful analytical concept than 'occupation', a point which highlights the increasing fluidity of movement *between* types of work rather than *within* single occupational/professional categories. At the same time, as Jones (Chapter 3) points out, a number of professional bodies are taking active steps to embed managerial skills into their training curricula, indicating that the nature of 'professionalism' is, at least in some cases, undergoing a transformation. The acquisition of managerial assets may no longer threaten professionals with the downgrading of their independent cognitive base by rooting them to a specific organization, as Savage *et al.* (1992) suggest, since the transformation from *organizational* to more footloose *managerial* assets loosens the importance of any particular context. It does, however, imply that there may be a growing division *within* professions as some acquire managerial assets while others eschew such developments. The uneven marketization of individual public services illustrates this emerging division (see the following section for further discussion of this point). For example, not all general practitioners have chosen to become total fundholders, nor have all schools applied for grant-maintained status.

To be fair, Savage *et al.* (1992) also suggest that the value of organizational assets may be on the wane, as part of a broader social shift away from mass production and mass consumption. As Fordist production systems break down, they suggest, traditional organizational hierarchies are being replaced by new ways of organizing; there is an emphasis on new skills and attributes (the ability to think strategically, see beyond perceived wisdoms and boundaries, to empower staff, etc.). This, they argue, is reducing the effectiveness of organizational assets and enhancing the position of professional specialists. While we clearly agree with the first contention, it is not so clear that it is professionals (in the traditional sense), backed by cultural assets – rather than managers (in the new sense) – who are benefiting from these changes. The analysis and interpretation of such developments need to be context-specific; that is, the relative advantage between professionals and managers will vary between and within professions and sectors. Thus it may equally be the case, as illustrated earlier, that the converse argument can be proposed.

Fragmentation of lateral solidarities
The points raised above question whether professionals, on the one hand, and managers, on the other, can really be distinguished through reference to a clearly defined and mutually exclusive set of 'assets'. However, while there is clearly evidence that the new 'managerial' assets are being acquired by both professionals *and* managers, this is not to say that all professionals and managers are choosing or are able, to follow this route. As the chapters by Jones and Menter and Muschamp show, there may be considerable resentment towards the encroaching managerialism from within the ranks of practising social workers and teachers. Similarly, Harrison shows, within medicine, that even the profound restructuring within the NHS has not led all (or even most) hospital doctors to embrace the new managerialism. This contrasts quite significantly with the research on general practitioners, who have generally been far more enthusiastic about taking on managerial roles and responsibilities. Halford and Leonard reiterate the point in terms of personal identities and the hostility with which teachers may view the managerialist trajectory within education. In sum, the chapters in this book suggest that the new managerialism within the public sector may result in the fragmentation of professional groups.

This evidence lends support to Friedson's (1994) suggestion that professions, as we have understood them, may lose their coherence (and thus perhaps their very definition) through internal processes of fragmentation (see Chapter 1). It is important to point out, however, that although managerialism may have had a precipitating effect upon the erosion of lateral solidarities, other factors have combined, in varying degrees, to have an additive impact. For example, technology has played a significant role in enabling the emergence of remote monitoring of professional work and the development of what Miller (1992) called the 'calculative self'. The use of technology has been differentially felt between professions. Some are more 'measurable' than others (see Harrison, Chapter 4) but all the sectors considered in this book have a high degree of heterogeneity, uncertainty and (organizational) complexity (Carter *et al.* 1992). Thus measurement of work performance becomes problematic. In short, the contribution of professions and professionals in social work, education and the health service is difficult to disentangle in assessing the overall outcome of these sectors. The problems in interpreting school or NHS league tables exemplify this. Other factors which have contributed, in varying degrees, to the erosion of lateral solidarities of professions include changing public attitudes to professionals, legislation enabling a challenge to the monopolistic practices of some professions (for example, the case of midwifery), and the role of the media in highlighting differences in provision and standards of service.

A significant development in managerialism during the last 20 years has been the ways in which managerialism, management and managers are no longer seen or treated as a homogeneous group. While it may be overstating the extent to which managers ever enjoyed a high degree of cohesion, the erosion of manager–manager lateral solidarities has been a notable impact of managerialism. Thus we should consider the wider impact upon all collective groups. Two broad issues emerge from an analysis of the erosion of managerial solidarities: managerial professionals and marketization.

First, we need to consider the impact upon lay or generic managers of the emergence of managerial professionals within all sectors (see Causer and Exworthy, Chapter 6). While professional lateral solidarities have been explored elsewhere, the consequences for lay managers have been less well investigated. Although not all professionals have acquired managerial assets, it is, nevertheless, a significant development in professional–managerial relations. It follows, however, that the power of lay managers will become less effective. Hunter (1992) argues that in the NHS this development may presage a situation similar to the one before managerialism was introduced: that is, professionals, by virtue of their acquisition of managerial assets, will enjoy the traditional benefits of their professional position *and* those of managerialism, such as access to negotiations and decisions regarding resource allocation. Managers, like 'administrators' before them, will, Hunter argues, become subordinate to professionals, especially doctors. Not all managers will be able to retain this former position in relation to managerial professionals. Given the rise of managerial professionals in the middle strata of schools and hospitals, etc., it is evident that managers also occupying this level will be most affected (Hoggett 1991).

Second, marketization, as argued throughout this book, has been a powerful influence upon the articulation between professionals and managers, especially since the late 1980s. The impact of marketization upon managerial solidarities has been differentially felt between sectors because some marketizations have been sector-wide (for example health care) whereas others have affected sub-sectors (for example education). Also, education has been somewhat different from social work and health care in that the managerial body has not been divided into two groups. In these other sectors, the institution of 'purchasers' and 'providers' has had the effect of creating a contractual separation between managers in formerly hierarchical organizations. Even if marketization becomes downplayed in future years, as might appear likely as a result of Labour government policy, the division between strategic and operational control (as key features of post-bureaucratic control – Hoggett 1991) appears to be readily accepted. The impact of the purchaser–provider split has been to erode the solidarities that did exist (or were assumed to exist) beforehand, a process which may not necessarily be halted, given central government policy.

In both these cases of solidarities between professionals and managers we have noted the ways in which the cohesion within the respective groups has eroded. However, it should not be assumed that the impact of this erosion necessarily precipitates the emergence of new forms of solidarity either within these groups or – possibly – between them. We recognize that, in effect, a 'vacuum' may occur in which new forms of solidarity have yet to be (fully) established. Such is the temporal perspective that we have taken that we cannot be certain that the forms we now see emerging have substance or durability. In other words, we may be seeing the fracturing or 'combustion' of lateral solidarities without their replacement by new forms. The result may be a network-like structure of loose affiliations and associations. The stratification associated with the development of, for example, work performance techniques applies equally well to professionals and managers, but the emergence of external auditors (as managerial professionals) (such as Ofsted inspectors) is too recent for us to be able to make lasting conclusions about new solidarities.

The consequences for the notion of 'equality of competence' appear to be closely linked to the development of work performance measures by managerial professionals and other managers. The impact will be to fragment still further professional stratification and to elevate the roles of the knowledge elite (see Harrison, Chapter 4, and Causer and Exworthy, Chapter 6). Overlaid on the template of purchasers and providers, the 'internal combustion' thesis appears to have some veracity although it should be noted that, like the deprofessionalization thesis, professional nemesis is often heralded but has yet to materialize.

The future

Speculating more specifically about the future direction of these professional–managerial relations is hazardous. The past, let alone the future, is not always clearly discernible. However, two trends appear to be especially noteworthy: the consequence of continued internal stratification of professions, and the impact of Labour policy following the 1997 general election.

First, increased emphasis on the evaluation of work performance and a greater role for the knowledge elite have been identified as crucial elements in the increased stratification of professions. Combined with the impact of managerialism in terms of increasing both the managerial components of all professional roles and the significance of managerial professionals, the direction would appear to be towards greater fragmentation or combustion. However, the demise of professional position and power which has been heralded for so long has as yet to come to fruition. Rather, intricate processes of reprofessionalization involving, among others, marketization and reinterpretation of professional competencies have been proposed here to denote an undercurrent in professional–managerial dynamics. Processes of reprofessionalization and deprofessionalization may be occurring simultaneously, which is having the effect of further exacerbating internal stratification.

Second, while many of the long-term societal trends have profound implications for the nature and directions of those interactions, changes in government also facilitate perhaps the most far-reaching changes. Thus the 1997 general election which brought Labour to power is highly significant for the public sector. Although Labour claim to accept the previous government's spending patterns – which presages some financial austerity – the ways in which much of this spending is implemented will be determined by the degree to which policies such as marketization, inspection and audit, and support for managerial policies, are continued and advanced. The direction which is to be taken has become increasingly clear since May 1997. Earlier statements are, nevertheless, useful indications since legislation has yet to be implemented. For instance, educational standards have emerged as a central policy area in which teachers and external inspectors are being given leading roles. The ways in which these 'new' relations will be played out is yet to emerge. Another example relates to the NHS. The December 1997 White Paper ('The new NHS: modern, dependable' – Cmd 3807) proposes to retain the distinction between operational and strategic functions while abolishing the 'internal market'. Also, the implications of this shift were heralded by Tony Blair, then leader of the Opposition, in speaking to the National Association of Health Authorities and Trusts 1996 annual conference. He said that 'The NHS needs to be well managed, and there are many dedicated and good managers. What concerns me are the excesses of the market and not the fact that we need skilled management to run the service' (quoted in the *Health Service Journal*, 27 June 1996: 12).

This highlights a possible Labour approach to professionals and managers, at least in the NHS and possibly in other public sector areas. Managers and managerialism are given implicit, if somewhat guarded, support. Recent plans to 'change the [NHS] internal market' may not be as far-reaching as some might have thought (or hoped for). For example, the intended policy (as of November 1997) is to establish, among others, longer-term 'agreements' (i.e. contracts). Thus elements of market mechanisms might persist following reorganization, although the market will operate differently from the period 1991–7.

This example of the NHS augurs a possible trend over the next few years in this and other public sector areas: namely, that managerialism will be accepted as a key government strategy for the implementation of local policy and that marketization will play a more limited role than hitherto. As such, we are likely to witness a continuation of many of the trends identified in this book, though they may be less pronounced than might have been expected.

In summary, therefore, the future of professional–managerial relations will be subject to profound social and policy influences at national and local levels. While the outcomes will everywhere be contingent to some extent, this book has provided a framework in which to view such developments. It has, therefore, not only tried to clarify the debate but to extend it. The challenge for us and others is to develop these cross-sectoral and cross-disciplinary studies of the interactions between professionals and managers.

References

Aaron, H.J. and Schwartz, W.B. (1984) *The Painful Prescription: Rationing Hospital Care*. Washington, DC: Brookings Institution.

Abbott, A. (1988) *The System of Professions*. London: University of Chicago Press.

Alaszewski, A. (1995) Restructuring health and welfare professions in the United Kingdom: the impact of internal markets on the medical, nursing and social work professions, in T. Johnson, G. Larkin and M. Saks (eds) *Health Professions and the State in Europe*. London: Routledge.

Alford, R.R. (1975) *Health Care Politics*. Chicago: University of Chicago Press.

Allsop, J. (1984) *Health Policy and the National Health Service*. London: Longman.

Apple, M. (1988) Work, class and teaching, in J. Ozga (ed.) *Schoolwork*. Milton Keynes: Open University Press.

Argyris, C. (1964) *Integrating the Individual and the Organization*. New York: Wiley.

Armstrong, D. (1990) Medicine as a profession: times of change, *British Medical Journal*, 301: 691–3.

Bagguley, P. (1991) Post-fordism and enterprise culture, in R. Keat and N. Abercrombie (eds) *Enterprise Culture*. London: Routledge.

Bailey, R. and Brake, M. (eds) (1975) *Radical Social Work*. London: Edward Arnold.

Baker, M.R. and Kirk, S. (eds) (1996) *Research and Development for the NHS: Evidence, Evaluation and Effectiveness*. Oxford: Radcliffe Medical Press.

Ball, S.J. (1987) *The Micro-Politics of the School: Towards a Theory of School Organization*. London: Methuen.

Ball, S. (1990) *Politics and Policy Making in Education*. London: Routledge.

Ball, S. (1994) *Education Reform: A Critical and Post-structural Approach*. Buckingham: Open University Press.

Bamford, T. (1982) *Managing Social Work*. London: Tavistock.

Bannatyne, K.V. (1902) The place and training of volunteers in charitable work, *Charity Organisation Review*, June: 332–47.

Barry, N. (1990) *Welfare*. Milton Keynes: Open University Press.

Bartlett, W. and Le Grand, J. (1993) The theory of quasi-markets, in J. Le Grand and W. Bartlett (eds) *Quasi-Markets and Social Policy*. Macmillan: London.

Bartlett, W., Propper, C., Wilson, D. and Le Grand, J. (eds) (1994) *Quasi-Markets in the Welfare State*. Bristol: School of Advanced Urban Studies.

Bates, M. and Kiersey, D.W. (1984) *Please Understand Me*. Del Mar, CA: Prometheus Nemesis Book Company.

Bauman, Z. (1996) From pilgrim to tourist: a short history of identity, in S. Hall and P. du Gay (eds) *Questions of Cultural Identity*. London: Sage.

Becker, S. and Silburn, R. (1990) *The New Poor Clients*. Wallington: Community Care.

Beynon, J. (1985) Institutional change and career histories in a comprehensive school, in S.J. Ball and I.F. Goodson (eds) *Teachers' Lives and Careers*. Lewes: The Falmer Press.

Birchall, J., Pollitt, C. and Putnam, K. (1995) Freedom to manage? The experience of NHS Trusts, grant maintained schools and voluntary transfers to public housing, paper presented to the Political Studies Association Annual Conference, University of York.

Bloor, G. and Dawson, P. (1994) Understanding professional culture in the organisational context, *Organisation Studies*, 15(2): 275–95.

Bolger, S., Corrigan, P., Docking, J. and Frost, N. (1981) *Towards Socialist Welfare Work*. London: Macmillan.

Boreham, P. (1983) Indetermination: professional knowledge, organization and control, *Sociological Review*, 31(4): 693–718.

Bosanquet, B. (1916) The philosophy of casework, *Charity Organisation Review*, 39: 117–38.

Bourdieu, P. (1990) *In Other Words*. Cambridge: Polity.

Bowe, R. and Ball, S. (1992) Doing what should come naturally: an exploration of LMS in one secondary school, in G. Wallace (ed.) *Local Management of Schools: Research and Experience*. Clevedon: Multilingual Matters.

Bowling, A. (1996) Health care rationing: the public's debate, *British Medical Journal*, 312: 670–4.

Brazier, M., Lovecy, J., Moran, M. and Potton, M. (1992) Falling from a tightrope? Doctors and lawyers between the market and the state, paper presented to Annual Conference of the Political Studies Association, University of Belfast.

Brewster, R. (1992) The new class? Managerialism and social work education and training, *Issues in Social Work Education*, 11(2): 81–93.

British Medical Association (1980) *The Handbook of Medical Ethics*. BMA: London.

Buck N., Devlin B. and Lunn, J.N. (1987) *Report of a Confidential Enquiry into Perioperative Deaths*. London: Nuffield Provincial Hospitals Trust.

Campbell, J. and Neill S.R.St.J. (1994a) *Primary Teachers at Work*. London: Routledge.

Campbell, J. and Neill, S.R.St.J. (1994b) *Curriculum Reform at Key Stage One*. Harlow: Longman/ATL.

Cannan, C. (1972) Social workers: training and professionalism, in T. Pateman (ed.) *Counter Course*. Harmondsworth: Penguin.

Cannan, C. (1994/5) Enterprise culture, professional socialisation and social work education in Britain, *Critical Social Policy*, 42(Winter): 5–18.

Carter, N., Klein, R. and Day, P. (1992) *How Organisations Measure Success*. London: Routledge.

Causer, G. and Jones, C. (1996a) Management and the control of technical labour, *Work, Employment and Society*, 10(1): 105–23.

Causer, G. and Jones, C. (1996b) One of them or one of us? The ambiguities of the professional as manager, in R. Fincham (ed.) *New Relationships in the Organized Professions*. Aldershot: Avebury.

CCETSW (1975) *Second Annual Report*. London: CCETSW.

Child, J. (1982) Professionals in the corporate world, in D. Dunkerley and G. Salaman (eds) *International Yearbook of Organization Studies 1981*. London: Routledge and Kegan Paul.

Clarke, J. (1996) After social work? in N. Parton (ed.) *Social Theory, Social Change and Social Work*. London: Routledge.

Clarke, J., Cochrane, J. and McLoughlin, E. (eds) (1994a) *Managing Social Policy*. London: Sage.

Clarke, J., Cochrane, A. and McLoughlin, E. (1994b) Mission accomplished or unfinished business? The impact of managerialization, in J. Clarke, A. Cochrane and E. McLoughlin (eds) *Managing Social Policy*. London: Sage.

Clegg, S. and Dunkerley, D. (1980) *Organization, Class, Control*. London: Routledge and Kegan Paul.

Coburn, D. (1992) Freidson then and now: an 'internalist' critique of Freidson's past and present views of the medical profession, *International Journal of Health Services*, 22(3): 497–512.

Cochrane, A. (1993) *Whatever Happened to Local Government?* Buckingham: Open University Press.

Cohen, A. (1994) *Self-Consiousness: An Alternative Anthropology of Identity*. London: Routledge.

Coyle, A. (1988) The limits of change: local government and equal opportunities for women, *Public Administration*, 67: 39–50.

Crang, P. (1994) It's showtime: on the workplace geographies of display in a restaurant in South East England, *Society and Space*, 12(6): 675–784.

Crompton, R. (1990) Professions in the current context, *Work, Employment and Society*, May: 147–66.

Curtis Committee (1946) *Report of the Care of Children's Committee*. London: HMSO.

Cutler, T. and Waine, B. (1994) *Managing the Welfare State*. Oxford: Berg.

Dandeker, C. (1990) *Surveillance, Power and Modernity*. Cambridge: Polity Press.

Davis, A. and Brook, E. (eds) (1985) *Women, the Family, and Social Work*. London: Tavistock Publications.

Davis, A. and Wainwright, S. (1996) Poverty work and the mental health services, *Breakthrough*, 1(1): 47–56.

Day, P. and Klein, R. (1983) The mobilisation of consent versus the management of conflict: decoding the Griffiths report, *British Medical Journal*, 287: 1813–15.

Deetz, S. (1992) Disciplinary power in the modern corporation, in M. Alvesson and H. Wilmott (eds) *Critical Management Studies*. London: Sage.

Dent, M. (1993) Professionalism, educated labour and the state: hospital medicine and the new managerialism, *Sociological Review*, 41(2): 244–73.

Department of Health (1991) *The Patient's Charter*. London: HMSO.

Department of Health and Social Security (1970) *The Future Structure of the National Health Service* (The Crossman Green Paper). London: HMSO.

Department of Health and Social Security (1972a) *National Health Service Reorganisation: England*, Cmnd. 5055. London: HMSO.

Department of Health and Social Security (1972b) *Management Arrangements for the Reorganised National Health Service*. London: HMSO.

Department of Health and Social Security and Welsh Office (1979) *Patients First: Consultative Paper on the Structure and Management of the National Health Service in England and Wales*. London: HMSO.

Department of Health, Welsh Office, Scottish Home and Health Department, and Northern Ireland Office (1989) *Working for Patients*, Cmnd. 555. London: HMSO.

Department of Health, Welsh Office and Scottish Office (1996) *Choice and Opportunity. Primary Care: The Future*, Cmnd. 3390. London: HMSO.

Dixon, G. and Glennerster, H. (1995) What do we know about fundholding in general practice? *British Medical Journal*, 311: 727–30.

Doehler, M. (1989) Physicians' professional autonomy in the welfare state: endangered or preserved? in G. Freddi and J.W. Bjorkman (eds) *Controlling Medical Professionals: The Comparative Politics of Health Governance*. New York: Sage.

du Gay, P. (1994) Making up managers, *British Journal of Sociology*, 45(4): 655–74.

du Gay, P. (1996a) *Consumption and Identity at Work*. London: Sage.

du Gay, P. (1996b) Organizing identity: entrepreneurial governance and public management, in S. Hall and P. du Gay (eds) *Questions of Cultural Identity*. London: Sage.

du Gay, P. (1996c) Organising identity: making up people at work, paper presented at the Southampton Space and Identity seminar series, May 1996.

Dunham, J. (1978) Change and stress in the head of department's role, *Educational Research*, 21(1): 44–8.

Dunleavy, P. (1982) Quasi-governmental sector professionalism, in A. Barker (ed.) *QUANGOs in Britain*. London: Macmillan.

Dunleavy, P. (1991) *Democracy, Bureaucracy and Public Choice*. Hemel Hempstead: Harvester Wheatsheaf.

Edgell, S. (1993) *Class*. London: Routledge.

Elliott, J. (1976) *Developing hypotheses about classrooms from teachers' practical constructs*. Ford Teaching Project. Cambridge: Cambridge Institute of Education.

Elston, M.A. (1991) The politics of professional power, in J. Gabe, M. Calnan and M. Bury (eds) *The Sociology of the Health Service*. London: Routledge.

Esland, G. (1980) Professions and professionalism, in G. Esland and G. Salaman (eds) *The Politics of Work and Occupations*. Milton Keynes: Open University Press.

Evans, R. and Russell, P. (1989) *The Creative Manager*. London: Unwin Hyman.

Evetts, J. (1993) LMS and headship: changing the contexts for micro-politics, *Educational Review*, 45(1): 53–65.

Exworthy, M. (1992) 'Central–local relations in the NHS: case-studies of decentralisation policies in community health services', unpublished PhD thesis. Department of Geography, Queen Mary and Westfield College, University of London.

Exworthy, M. (1994) The contest for control in community health services: professionals and managers dispute decentralisation, *Policy and Politics*, 22(1): 17–29.

Exworthy, M. (1995) *Purchasing Clinical Audit*, research paper, University of Southampton: Institute for Health Policy Studies.

Farnham, D. and Horton, S. (1996) *Managing the New Public Services*. Basingstoke: Macmillan.

Ferguson, K.E. (1984) *The Feminist Case Against Bureaucracy*. Philadelphia, PA: Temple University Press.

Ferlie, E., Ashburner, L., Fitzgerald., L. and Pettigrew, A. (1996) *The New Public Management in Action*. Oxford: Oxford University Press.

Fielding, A.G. and Portwood, D. (1980) Professions and the state, *Sociological Review*, 28(1): 25–53.

Fitz, J., Halpin, D. and Power, S. (1993) *Grant-Maintained Schools: Education in the Marketplace*. London: Kogan Page.

Fitzgerald, L. (1991) Made to measure, *Health Service Journal*, 31 October: 24–5.

Flynn, N. (1990) *Public Sector Management*. Hemel Hempstead: Harvester Wheatsheaf.

Flynn, N. (1994) Control, commitment, contracts, in J. Clarke, A. Cochrane and E. McLoughlin (eds) *Managing Social Policy*. London: Sage.

Flynn, R. (1988) *Cutback Management in Health Services*. Salford: University of Salford, Department of Sociology and Anthropology.

Flynn, R. (1992) *Structures of Control in Health Management*. London: Routledge.

Flynn, R. (1997) Quasi-welfare, associationalism and the social division of citizenship, *Citizenship Studies*, 1(3): 335–50.

Flynn, R., Williams, G. and Pickard, S. (1995) Contracts and the quasi-market in community health services, *Journal of Social Policy*, 24: 4.

Flynn, R., Williams, G. and Pickard, S. (1996) *Markets and Networks: Contracting in Community Health Services*. Buckingham: Open University Press.

Ford, P. (1996) Competences; their use and misuse, in P. Ford and P. Hayes (eds) *Educating for Social Work: Arguments for Optimism*. Aldershot: Avebury.

Foster, J. (1987) Women on the wane, *Insight*, 2(45): 15–17.

Foster, J. (1988) On the hop, *Insight*, 3(21): 20–1.

Fox, A. (1974) *Beyond Contract*. London: Faber and Faber.

Franklin, B. (1989) Wimps and bullies: press reporting of child abuse, in P. Carter, T. Jeffs and M. Smith (eds) *Social Work and Social Welfare Yearbook I*. Milton Keynes: Open University Press.

Freedman, S. (1988) Teacher 'burnout' and institutional stress, in J. Ozga (ed.) *Schoolwork*. Milton Keynes: Open University Press.

Freemantle, N. and Harrison, S. (1993) Interleukin 2: the public and professional face of rationing in the NHS, *Critical Social Policy*, 13(3): 94–117.

Freidson, E. (1970) *Professional Dominance*. New York: Altherton Press.

Freidson, E. (1985) The reorganisation of the medical profession, *Medical Care Review*, 42(1): 11–35.

Freidson, E. (1986) *Professional Powers*. Chicago: University of Chicago Press.

Freidson, E. (1994) *Professionalism Re-Born: Theory, Prophecy and Policy*. Oxford: Polity Press.

Garrett, A. (1949) Historical survey of the evolution of casework, *Journal of Social Casework*, 30(6): 219–29.

Gergen, K.J. (1992) Organization theory in the postmodern era, in M. Reed and M. Hughes (eds) *Rethinking Organization: New Directions in Organization Theory and Analysis*. London: Sage.

Giddens, A. (1991a) *Modernity and Self-identity*. Cambridge: Polity Press.

Giddens, A. (1991b) *The Consequences of Modernity*. Cambridge: Polity Press.

Giles, S. (1993) Rationing scheme will exclude minor illnesses from NHS, *Health Service Journal*, 26 August: 7.

Glastonbury, B. (1975) The social worker: cannon fodder in the age of administration, *Social Work Today*, 6(10).

Glastonbury, B., Cooper, D.M. and Hawkins, P. (1980) *Social Work in Conflict: The Practitioner and the Bureaucrat*. London: Croom Helm.

Glennerster, H. (1995) *British Social Policy Since 1945*. Oxford: Blackwell.

Glennerster, H., Matsaganis, M., Owens, P. and Hancock, S. (1994) *Implementing GP Fundholding: Wild Card or Winning Hand?* Buckingham: Open University Press.

Goffman, E. (1969) *The Presentation of Self in Everyday Life*. London: Penguin.

Goodson, I.F. (1981) Life histories and the study of schooling, *Interchange*, 11(4): 62–76.

Goodwin, N. and Pinch, S. (1995) Explaining geographical variations in the contracting out of NHS hospital ancillary services: a contextual approach, *Environment and Planning A*, 27: 1397–418.

Gordon, C. (1987) The soul of the citizen: Max Weber and Michel Foucault on rationality and government, in S. Whimster and S. Lash (eds) *Max Weber: Rationality and Modernity*. London: Allen and Unwin.

Grace, G. (1995) *School Leadership*. London: Falmer.

Gray, A. and Jenkins, W. (1994) Markets, managers and public service, in P. Taylor-Gooby and R. Lawson (eds) *Markets and Managers*. Buckingham: Open University Press.

Groenewegen, P.P. and Calnan, M. (1995) Changes in the control of health care systems in Europe: implications for professional autonomy, *European Journal of Public Health*, 5(4): 240–4.

Hacking, I. (1986) Making up people, in T. Heller, M. Sosna and D. Wellbery (eds) *Reconstructing Individualism: Autonomy, Individuality and the Self in Western Thought*. Stanford, CA: Stanford University Press.

Hadley, R. and Clough, R. (1996) *Care in Chaos*. London: Cassell.

Halford, S. and Savage, M. (1995) Changing organisations, changing people? Gender and cultural change in banking and local government, *Work, Employment and Society*, 9(1): 92–122.

Halford, S. and Savage, M. (1997) Rethinking restructuring: embodiment, agency and identity in organisational change, in R. Lee and J. Wills (eds) *Geographies of Economies*. London: Edward Arnold.

Halford, S., Savage, M. and Witz, A. (1997) *Gender, Careers and Organisations: Current Developments in Banking, Nursing and Local Government*. Basingstoke: Macmillan.

Hall, S. (1996) Who needs identity? in S. Hall and P. du Gay (eds) *Questions of Cultural Identity*. London: Sage.

Hall, V., Mackay, H. and Morgan, C. (1986) *Headteachers at Work*. Milton Keynes: Open University Press.

Ham, C.J. (1994) *Management and Competition in the New NHS*. Oxford: Radcliffe Medical Press.

Hampton, J.R. (1983) The end of clinical freedom, *British Medical Journal*, 287(6401): 1237–8.

Hargreaves, A. (1994) *Changing Teachers, Changing Times: Teachers' Work and Culture in the Postmodern Age*. London: Cassell.

Harrison, S. (1981) The politics of health manpower, in A.F. Long and G. Mercer (eds) *Manpower Planning in the National Health Service*. Farnborough: Gower Press.

Harrison, S. (1982) Consensus decisionmaking in the National Health Service: a review, *Journal of Management Studies*, 19(4): 377–94.

Harrison, S. (1988) *Managing the National Health Service: Shifting the Frontier?* London: Chapman and Hall.

Harrison, S. (1994a) Knowledge into practice: what's the problem? *Journal of Management in Medicine*, 8(2): 9–16.

Harrison, S. (1994b) *Health Service Management in the 1980s: Policymaking on the Hoof?* Aldershot: Avebury.

Harrison, S. (1996) Evidence-based medicine: policy, politics and problems, *Contemporary Political Studies*, 3: 1133–40.

Harrison, S. and Pollitt, C.J. (1994) *Controlling Health Professionals*. Buckingham: Open University Press.

Harrison, S. and Schultz, R.I. (1989) Clinical autonomy in the U.K. and the U.S.A. Contrasts and convergence, in G. Freddi and J.W. Bjorkman (eds) *Controlling Medical Professionals: The Comparative Politics of Health Governance*. London: Sage.

Harrison, S. and Wistow, G. (1992) The purchaser/provider split in English health care: towards explicit rationing? *Policy and Politics*, 20(2): 123–30.

Harrison, S. and Hunter, D.J. (1994) *Rationing Health Care: Options for Public Policy*. London: Institute of Public Policy Research.

Harrison, S., Pohlman, C.E. and Mercer, G. (1984) Concepts of clinical freedom amongst English physicians, paper presented at EAPHSS Conference on Clinical Autonomy, London: King's Fund Centre.

Harrison, S., Hunter, D. and Pollitt, C. (1990) *The Dynamics of British Health Policy*. Unwin Hyman: London.

Harrison, S., Hunter, D.J., Marnoch, G. and Pollitt, C. (1992) *Just Managing: Power and Culture in the National Health Service*. London: Macmillan.

Hegelson, S. (1990) *The Female Advantage: Women's Ways of Leadership*. New York: Doubleday/Currency.

Heginbotham, C. (1993) Health care priority setting: a survey of doctors, managers and the general public, in R. Smith (ed.) *Rationing in Action*. London: BMJ Publishing Group.

Hinings, C.R., Hickson, D.J., Pennings, J.M. and Schneck, R.E. (1971) Structural conditions of intra-organisational power, *Administrative Science Quarterly*, 16(2) June: 147–59.

Hoffenberg, R. (1987) *Clinical Freedom*. London: Nuffield Provincial Hospitals Trust.

Hoggett, P. (1987) Farewell to mass production? in P. Hoggett and R. Hambleton (eds) *Decentralisation and Democracy*. Bristol: School for Advanced Urban Studies.

Hoggett, P. (1990) *Modernisation, Political Strategy and the Welfare State*, working paper, Bristol: School for Advanced Urban Studies.

Hoggett, P. (1991) A new management in the public sector? *Policy and Politics*, 19(4): 243–56.

Hoggett, P. (1994) The politics of modernisation of the UK welfare state, in R. Burrows and B. Loader (eds) *Towards a Post-Fordist Welfare State?* London: Routledge.

Hoggett, P. (1996) New modes of control in the public service, *Public Administration*, 74: 9–32.

Holman, B. (1993) *A New Deal for Social Welfare*. Oxford: Lion.

Hood, C. (1991) A public management for all seasons? *Public Administration*, 69(Spring): 3–19.

Hood, C. (1995a) Contemporary public management: a new global paradigm? *Public Policy and Administration*, 10(2): 104–17.

Hood, C. (1995b) The new public management in the 1980s: variations on a theme, *Accounting Organizations and Society*, 20(2/3): 93–109.

Huckman, L. and Fletcher, J. (1996) A question of costs: budget management in secondary schools, in C.J. Pole and R. Chawla-Duggan (eds) *Reshaping Education in the 1990s: Perspectives on Secondary Schooling*. London: Falmer Press.

Hunter, D.J. (1992) Doctors as managers: poachers turned gamekeepers? *Social Science and Medicine*, 35(4): 557–66.

Hunter, D.J. (1994) From tribalism to corporatism: the managerial challenge to medical dominance, Chapter 1 in J. Gabe, D. Kelleher and G. William (eds) *Challenging Medicine*. London: Routledge.

Irvine, E.E. (1954) Research into problem families, *British Journal of Psychiatric Social Work*, 9 (Spring): 24–33.

Jessop, B. (1991a) Thatcherism and flexibility, in B. Jessop, H. Kastendiek, K. Nielsen and O. Pedersen (eds) *The Politics of Flexibility*. Aldershot: Edward Elgar.

Jessop, B. (1991b) The welfare state in the transition from Fordism to post-Fordism, in B. Jessop, H. Kastendiek, K. Nielsen and O. Pedersen (eds) *The Politics of Flexibility*. Aldershot: Edward Elgar.

Jessop, B. (1994) The transition to post-Fordism and the Schumpeterian workfare state, in R. Burrows and B. Loader (eds) *Towards a Post-Fordist Welfare State?* London: Routledge.

Johnston, J. (1994) Extra-contractual referrals: squaring the circle, in S. Harrison and N. Freemantle (eds) *Working for Patients: Early Research Findings*. Leeds: University of Leeds, Nuffield Institute for Health.

Johnson, T. (1972) *Professions and Power*. London: Macmillan.

Johnson, T.J. (1993) Expertise and the state, in M. Gane and T.J. Johnson (eds) *Foucault's New Domains*. London: Routledge.

Johnson, T. (1995) Governmentality and the institutionalisation of expertise, in T. Johnson, G. Larkin and M. Saks (eds) *Health Professions and the State in Europe*. London: Routledge.

Jones, C. (1983) *State Social Work and the Working Class*. London: Macmillan.

Jones, C. (1989) The end of the road? Issues in social work education, in P. Carter, T. Jeffs and M. Smith (eds) *Social Work and Social Welfare Yearbook I*. Milton Keynes: Open University Press.

Jones, C. (1996a) Anti-intellectualism and the peculiarities of British social work education, in N. Parton (ed.) *Social Theory, Social Change and Social Work*. London: Routledge.

Jones, C. (1996b) Regulating social work: a review of the review, in S. Jackson and M. Preston Shoot (eds) *Educating Social Workers in a Changing Policy Context*. London: Whiting and Birch.

Jones, C. (1997) The case against CCETSW, *Issues in Social Work Education*, 17(1): 53–64.

Jones, C. and Novak, T. (1993) Social work today, *British Journal of Social Work*, 23(3): 195–212.

Jones, P.R. (1981) *Doctors in the BMA: A Case Study in Collective Action*. Farnborough: Gower.

Kendall, K. (1972) Dream or nightmare? The future of social work education, *Social Work Today*, 3(16): 2–8.

King, D. (1987) *The New Right*. London: Macmillan.

Klein, R. (1989) *The Politics of the NHS*. Harlow: Longman.

Klein, R. (1990) The state and the profession: the politics of the double bed, *British Medical Journal*, 301: 700–2.

Langan, M. and Clarke, J. (1994) Managing in the mixed economy of care, in J. Clarke, A. Cochrane and E. McLaughlin (eds) *Managing Social Policy*. London: Sage.

Laplanche, J. and Pontalis, J. (1985) *The Language of Psychoanalysis*. London: Hogarth Press.

Larkin, G.V. (1983) *Occupational Monopoly and Modern Medicine*. London: Tavistock.

Larson, M.S. (1990) In the matter of experts and professionals, or how impossible it is to leave nothing unsaid, in R. Torstendahl and M. Burrage (eds) *The Formation of Professions*. London: Sage.

Lash, S. and Urry, J. (1987) *The End of Organised Capitalism*. Cambridge: Polity Press.

Lawn, M. and Ozga, J. (1988) The educational worker? A reassessment of teachers, in J. Ozga (ed.) *Schoolwork*. Milton Keynes: Open University Press.

Leach, S., Stewart, J. and Walsh, K. (1994) *The Changing Organisation and Management of Local Government*. Basingstoke: Macmillan.

Le Grand, J. (1990) *Quasi-markets and Social Policy*. Bristol: School for Advanced Urban Studies.

Le Grand, J. (1994) Evaluating the NHS reforms, in R. Robinson and J. Le Grand (eds) *Evaluating the NHS Reforms*. Hermitage: Policy Journals.

Le Grand, J. and Bartlett, W. (eds) (1993) *Quasi-markets and Social Policy*. London: Macmillan.

Leinberger, P. and Tucker, B. (1991) *The New Individualists: The Generation After The Organization Man*. New York: Harper Collins.

Leonard, P. (1995) 'Gender/organization/representation: a critical and poststructuralist approach to gender and organizational theory', unpublished PhD thesis. University of Southampton.

Leonard, P. (1998) Gendering change? Management, masculinity and the dynamics of incorporation, *Gender and Education*, 10(1): 71–84.

Levačić, R. (1995) *Local Management of Schools: Analysis and Practice*. Buckingham: Open University Press.

Lindblom, C.E. (1979), Still muddling, not yet through, *Public Administration Review*, 39(6): 517–26.

Lipsky, M. (1976) Toward a theory of street-level bureaucracy, in W. Hawley and M. Lipsky (eds) *Theoretical Perspectives on Urban Policy*. Englewood Cliffs, NJ: Prentice Hall.

Lipsky, M. (1980) *Street-Level Bureaucracy*. New York: Russell Sage Foundation.

Lipsky, M. (1991) The paradox of managing discretionary works in social welfare policy, in M. Adler, C. Bell, J. Clasen and A. Sinfield (eds) *The Sociology of Social Security*. Edinburgh University Press: Edinburgh.

Lloyd, C. and Seifert, R. (1995) Restructuring in the NHS: the impact of the 1990s reforms on the management of labour, *Work, Employment and Society*, 9(2): 359–78.

Lukes, S. (1974) *Power: A Radical View*. London: Macmillan.

Lupton, C. (1992) Feminism, managerialism and performance management, in M. Langan and L. Day (eds) *Women's Oppression and Social Work*. London: Routledge.

Macdonald, K. (1995) *The Sociology of the Professions*. London: Sage.

MacIver, R.M. (1931) *The Contribution of Sociology to Social Work*. New York: Columbia University Press.

Mackay, L. (1993) *Conflicts in Care: Medicine and Nursing*. London: Chapman and Hall.

Mackintosh Committee (1951) *Report of the Committee on Social Workers in the Mental Health Service*. London: HMSO.

Marshall, J. (1984) *Women Managers: Travellers in a Male World*. Chichester: John Wiley.

Marshall, T.H. (1946) Training for social work, in Nuffield College (ed.) *Training for Social Work*. London: Oxford University Press.

Maw, J. (1994) The deputy head's role under local management of schools, paper presented to the Annual Conference of the British Educational Research Association, Oxford, September.

Maychell, K. (1994) *Counting the Cost: The Impact of LMS on Schools' Patterns of Spending*. Slough: National Foundation for Educational Research.

McKinlay, J.B. and Arches, J. (1985) Towards the proletarianisation of physicians, *International Journal of Health Services*, 15: 161–95.

Mechanic, D. (1991) Sources of countervailing power in medicine, *Journal of Health Politics, Policy and Law*, 16(3): 485–98.

Menter, I. with Muschamp, Y., Nicholls, P., Ozga, J. and Pollard, A. (1995) Still carrying the can: primary school headship in the 1990s, *School Organisation*, 15(3): 301–12.

Menter, I., Muschamp, Y., Nicholls, P., Ozga, J. and Pollard, A. (1997) *Work and Identity in the Primary School: A Post-fordist Analysis*. Buckingham: Open University.

Merton, R. (1957) *Social Theory and Social Structure*. New York: The Free Press.

Miller, P. (1992) Accounting and objectivity: the invention of calculating selves and calculating spaces, *Annals of Scholarship*, 9(1/2): 61–86.

Miller, P. (1994) Accounting as social and institutional practice: an introduction, in A. Hopwood and P. Miller (eds) *Accounting as Social and Institutional Practice*. Cambridge: Cambridge University Press.

Miller, P. and Rose, N. (1988) The Tavistock programme: the government of subjectivity and social life, *Sociology*, 22(2): 171–92.

Ministry of Health and Department of Health for Scotland (1944) *A National Health Service* Cmnd 6502. London: HMSO.

Mohan, J. (1995) *A National Health Service? The Restructuring of Health Care in Britain since 1979*. Basingstoke: Macmillan.

Moore, W. (1995) Is doctors' power shrinking? *Health Service Journal*, 9 November: 24–7.

Moran, M. and Wood, B. (1993) *States, Regulation and the Medical Profession*. Buckingham: Open University Press.

Morgan, G. (1993) *Imaginization: The Art of Creative Management*. Newbury Park, CA: Sage.

Murphy, R. (1990) Proletarianization or bureaucratization: the fall of the professional? in R. Torstendahl and R. Burrage (eds) *The Formation of Professions*. London: Sage.

NALGO (1989) *Social Work in Crisis*. London: NALGO.

Navarro, V. (1988) Professional dominance or proletarianisation? Neither, *Millbank Quarterly*, 66: 57–75.

Newman, J. and Clarke, J. (1994) Going about our business? in J. Clarke, A. Cochrane and E. McLoughlin (eds) *Managing Social Policy*. London: Sage.

NHS Executive (1996a) *Priorities and Planning: Guidelines for the NHS*. London: Department of Health.

NHS Executive (1996b) *Clinical Guidelines: Using Clinical Guidelines to Improve Patient Care Within the NHS*. London: Department of Health.

NHS Management Executive (1993) *The Nurse Executive Director Post*. Leeds: NHS Management Executive.

Nias, J. (1985) Reference groups in primary teaching: talking, listening and identity, in S.J. Ball and I.F. Goodson (eds) *Teachers' Lives and Careers*. Lewes: The Falmer Press.

Nias, J. (1989) *Primary Teachers Talking: A Study of Teaching as Work*. London: Routledge.

Nippert-Eng, C.E. (1996) *Home and Work: Negotiating Boundaries through Everyday Life*. Chicago: University of Chicago Press.

O'Connor, J. (1973) *The Fiscal Crisis of the State*. New York: St. Martin's Press.

Offe, C. (1984) *Contradictions of the Welfare State*. London: Hutchinson.

Otway, O. (1996) Social work with children and families: from child welfare to child protection, in N. Parton (ed.) *Social Theory, Social Change and Social Work*. London: Routledge.

Ozga, J. (ed.) (1993) *Women in Educational Management*. Buckingham: Open University Press.

Ozga, J. and Lawn, M. (1981) *Teachers, Professionalism and Class*. Lewes: Falmer Press.

Packwood T., Keen J. and Buxton M. (1991), *Hospitals in Transition: The Resource Management Experiment*. Buckingham: Open University Press.

Packwood, T., Keen, J. and Buxton, M. (1992) Process and structure: resource management and the development of sub-unit organisational structure, *Health Services Management Research*, 5(1): 66–76.

Pahl, R., Flynn, R. and Buck, N. (1983) *Structures and Processes of Urban Life*. London: Longman.

Painter, J. (1991) The geography of trade union responses to local government privatisation, *Transactions of the Institute of British Geographers*, 16(2): 214–26.

Parton, N. (1991) *Governing the Family*. Basingstoke: Macmillan.

Payne, M. (1995) *Social Work and Community Care*. Basingstoke: Macmillan.

Penley, S. (1946) Practical training for social work, *Social Work*, 3(11): 265–8.

Petchey, R. (1995) General practitioner fundholding: weighing the evidence, *The Lancet*, 346: 1139–42.

Pinch, S. (1997) *Worlds of Welfare*. London: Routledge.

Pithouse, A. (1987) *Social Work: The Social Organisation of an Invisible Trade*. Aldershot: Avebury.

Pollard, A., Broadfoot, P., Croll, P., Osborne, M. and Abbot, D. (1994) *Changing English Primary Schools?* London: Cassell.

Pollitt, C. (1993) Audit and accountability: the missing dimension? *Journal of the Royal Society of Medicine*, 86 (April): 209–11.

Pollitt, C. (1984) Professionals and public policy, *Public Administration Bulletin*, 44: 29–46.

Pollitt, C. (1990) *Managerialism and the Public Services*. Oxford: Blackwell.

Poole, M., Mansfield, R., Martinez-Lucio, M. and Turner, B. (1995) Change and continuities within the public sector: contrasts between public and private sector managers in Britain, the effects of the Thatcher years, *Public Administration* 73 (Summer): 271–86.

Power, S., Halpin, D. and Fitz, J. (1996) The grant maintained schools policy: the English experience of educational self-governance, in C.J. Pole and R. Chawla-Duggan (eds) *Reshaping Education in the 1990s: Perspectives on Secondary Schooling*. Lewes: Falmer Press.

Price, D. (1996) Lessons for health care rationing from the case of Child B, *British Medical Journal*, 312: 167–9.

Pringle, R. (1989) *Secretaries Talk*. London: Verso.

Proctor, N. (ed.) (1990) *The Aims of Primary Education and the National Curriculum*. Lewes: Falmer Press.

Propper, C., Bartlett, W. and Wilson, D. (1994) Introduction, in W. Bartlett, C. Propper, D. Wilson and J. Le Grand (eds) *Quasi-Markets in the Welfare State*. Bristol: School for Advanced Urban Studies.

Ray, L. and Reed, M. (1994) Max Weber and the dilemmas of modernity, in L. Ray and M. Reed (eds) *Organizing Modernity*. London: Routledge.

Reed, M. (1989) *The Sociology of Management*. Hemel Hempstead: Harvester Wheatsheaf.

Reed, M. (1993) Organizations and modernity, in J. Hassard and M. Parker (eds) *Postmodernism and Organizations*. London: Sage.

Reed, M. and Anthony, P. (1992) Professionalising management and managing professionalisation: British management in the 1980s, *Journal of Management Studies*, 29(5): 591–613.

Ribbins, P. (1985) The role of the middle manager in the secondary school, in M. Hughes, P. Ribbins and H. Thomas (eds) *Managing Education: The System and the Institution*. London: Holt, Rinehart and Winston.

Richan, W.C. and Mendelsohn, A.R. (1973) *Social Work: The Unloved Profession*. New York: New Viewpoints.

Rosener, J.F. (1990) Ways Women Lead, *Harvard Business Review*, November–December: 119–25.

Rueschemeyer, D. (1983) Professional autonomy and the social control of expertise, in R. Dingwall and P. Lewis (eds) *The Sociology of the Professions*. London: Macmillan.

Saks, M. (1995) *Professions and the Public Interest*. London: Routledge.

Salaman, G. (1982) Managing the frontier of control, in A. Giddens and G. Mackenzie (eds) *Social Class and the Division of Labour*. Cambridge: Cambridge University Press.

Saunders, P. (1986) *Social Theory and the Urban Question*. London: Hutchinson.

Savage, M., Barlow, J., Dickens, P. and Fielding, A. (1992) *Property, Bureaucracy and Culture: Middle Class Formation in Contemporary Britain*. London: Routledge.

Scase, R. and Goffee, R. (1989) *Reluctant Managers: Their Work and Lifestyles*. London: Routledge.

Schorr, A. (1992) *The Personal Social Services: An Outsider's View*. York: Rowntree Foundation.

Schulz, R.I. and Harrison, S. (1986) Physician autonomy in the Federal Republic of Germany, Great Britain, and the United States, *International Journal of Health Planning and Management*, 1(5): 335–55.

Scott, J. (1985) *Corporations, Classes and Capitalism*. London: Hutchinson.

Scrivens, E. (1988) The management of clinicians in the National Health Service, *Social Policy and Administration*, 22(1): 22–34.

Simpkin, M. (1979) *Trapped Within Welfare*. London: Macmillan.

Stoker, G. (1989) Creating a local government for a post-fordist society, in J. Stewart and G. Stoke (eds) *The Future of Local Government*. Basingstoke: Macmillan.

Stoker, G. (1990) Regulation theory, local government and the transition from fordism, in D. King and J. Pierre (eds) *Challenges to Local Government*. London: Sage.

Tanenbaum, S.J. (1994) Knowing and acting in medical practice: the epistemological politics of outcomes research, *Journal of Health Politics, Policy and Law*, 19(1): 27–44.

Taylor-Gooby, P. (1991) *Social Change, Social Welfare and Social Science*. Hemel Hempstead: Harvester Wheatsheaf.

Taylor-Gooby, P. (1994) Postmodernism and social policy – a great leap backwards? *Journal of Social Policy*, 23(3): 385–404.

Taylor-Gooby, P. and Lawson, R. (1994) Where do we go from here? in P. Taylor-Gooby and R. Lawson (eds) *Markets and Managers*. Buckingham: Open University Press.

Thompson, G., Frances, J., Levačić, R. and Mitchell, J. (1991) Introduction, in G. Thompson *et al.* (eds) *Markets, Hierarchies and Networks*. London: Sage.

Tolliday, H. (1978) Clinical autonomy, in E. Jaques (ed.) *Health Services: Their Nature and Organisation and the Role of Patients, Doctors, and the Health Professions*. London: Heinemann.

Tongue, R. (1993) Financial management, in D. Farnham and S. Horton (eds) *Managing the New Public Services*. Basingstoke: Macmillan.

Townsend, P. *et al.* (eds) (1970) *The Fifth Social Service*. London: Fabian Society.

Underwood Report (1955) *Report of the Committee on Maladjusted Children*. London: HMSO.

Vinnicombe, S. (1987) What exactly are the differences in female and male working styles? *Women in Management Review*, 3(1): 13–21.

Walby, S. and Greenwell, J. (1994) Managing the National Health Service, Chapter 3 in J. Clarke, A. Cochran and E. Mclaughlin (eds) *Managing Social Policy*. London: Sage.

Walby, S. and Greenwell, J., with Mackay, L. and Soothill, K. (1994) *Medicine and Nursing: Professions in a Changing Health Service*. London: Sage.

Wallace, M. (1992) Coping with multiple innovation: an exploratory study, *School Organisation*, 11(2): 187–209.

Walsh, K. (1995) *Public Services and Market Mechanisms*. Basingstoke: Macmillan.

Watkin, B. (1975) *Documents on Health and Social Services: 1834 to the Present Day*. London: Methuen.

Webb, D. (1996) Regulation for radicals: the state, CCETSW and the academy, in N. Parton (ed.) *Social Theory, Social Change and Social Work*. London: Routledge.

Whitty, G. (1989) The new right and the national curriculum: state control or market forces? in M. Flude and M. Hammer (eds) *The Education Reform Act 1988*. Lewes: The Falmer Press.

Whyte, W. (1957) *The Organization Man*. New York: Touchstone.

Wilding, P. (1982) *Professional Power and Social Welfare*. London: Routledge and Kegan Paul.

Williams, B. (1996) *Freedom on Probation*. London: Association of University Teachers.

Williamson, P.J. (1990) *General Management in the Scottish Health Service*. Aberdeen: University of Aberdeen Department of Community Medicine.

Witz, A. (1992) *Professions and Patriarchy*. London: Routledge.

Wood, S. (1989) New wave management? *Work, Employment and Society*, 3(3): 379–402.

Woods, P. (1981) Strategies, commitment and identity: making and breaking the teacher, in L. Marton and S. Walker (eds) *Schools, Teachers and Teaching*. Lewes: The Falmer Press.

Woods, P.A., Bagley, C. and Glatter, R. (1996) Dynamics of competition – the effects of local competitive arenas on schools, in C.J. Poles and R. Chawla-Duggan (eds) *Reshaping Education in the 1990s: Perspectives on Secondary Schools.* Lewes: The Falmer Press.

Index